Boho
EMBROIDERY

THE PATTERN COLLECTION

Over 30 Modern Motifs &
20 Traditional Stitches

NICHOLE VOGELSINGER

Published in 2018 by
Lucky Spool Media, LLC
www.luckyspool.com
info@luckyspool.com

Text © Nichole Vogelsinger
Editor: Susanne Woods
Designer: Rae Ann Spitzenberger
Illustrator: Kari Vojtechovsky
Embroidery Illustrator: Alison Glass
Photographer: Holly DeGroot

9 8 7 6 5 4 3 2 1
First Edition
Printed in China

Library of Congress Cataloging-in-Publication Data available upon request
ISBN 978-1-940655-32-1
LSID0042

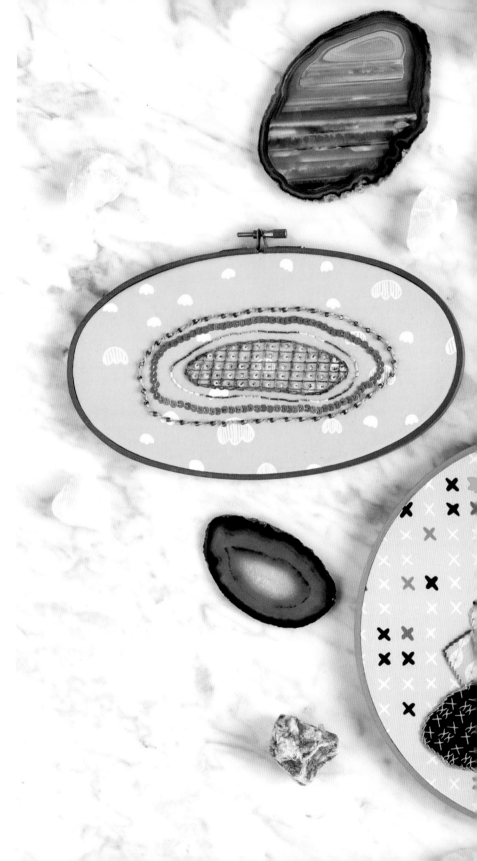

CONTENTS

DEDICATION

This book is dedicated to my parents, sister and brother for all of your love and support. To my boys for being so patient and understanding and being my constant cheerleaders. Keep being shiny! -ILY heart- And to Bix for all that I can't even put into words… I hear exclamation points (!!!) are the new comma splices. Love you!

ACKNOWLEDGMENTS

Thank you to Sue and Kelly at Sue Spargo and Kelly at Sulky for the beautiful threads I used throughout this book. A huge thank you to Daryl and Giuseppe at Andover Fabrics and Demi at RJR Fabrics for so many of the fabrics that I used for the projects in this book. Another huge thanks to Amy Reber for going above and beyond to provide me with fabric from an unreleased collection! And an even bigger thank you to Danielle for jumping right in to help me out with all of my braiding needs!

To the amazing Lucky Spool team, and especially Susanne Woods, for once again helping me to create a book that was exactly as I envisioned it!

BOHO iS BACK!

I'm so excited to take another journey with all of you lovely stitchers who are interested in embracing the free-spiritedness that comes with Boho embroidery.

This follow-up to *Boho Embroidery: Modern Projects from Traditional Stitches* will take your stitching further and have you exploring textures both in the stitches you create and the materials you use. I encourage you to think beyond your typical embroidery thread and pre-printed patterns and expand your repertoire with new stitches, a variety of threads and adaptable patterns.

Speaking of patterns, you might think it odd that this book contains a collection of patterns and yet I'm encouraging you to break from printed patterns! The patterns that are contained within these pages are inspired by flora and fauna and the colors and shapes found in everyday life. You have the choice to follow the patterns exactly as they are or — and

I encourage this — take the patterns and tailor them to your own style.

Boho embroidery is about taking embroidery know-how and creating something new that feels fresh and modern and reflects and embraces your own style. The world would be a boring place if we all simply imitated the art that inspired us. Make it new — do not be afraid to experiment and take chances with what you create. Maybe it will work, maybe it will look horrible, but either way you will learn from trying new things and forging your own distinct path in this craft.

When I teach embroidery workshops, the most common comment I hear from stitchers is that freeform Boho embroidery has inspired them to pick up the craft after many years of not embroidering. Non-stitchers with a background in other art forms tell me they now want to take on this craft. I hope the same will be true for you.

Enjoy this journey and happy stitching!

CHAPTER 1

Expanding Your Embroidery

TOOL KiT

BASIC EMBROIDERY SUPPLIES

The basic supplies that you need to begin embroidering are relatively few and simple: an embroidery hoop, needle, scissors, fabric, and some thread. And that's it!

However, like an oil painter might begin with a palette that consists of just a few tubes of inexpensive paint colors and then she gradually adds to that palette, maybe even buying more expensive paints as she better understands what works for her art, an embroidery artist's palette will grow along with her skills.

As you experiment with a variety of stitches, you may want to add new and interesting materials to your repertoire. Use them to keep your work fresh and keep you feeling excited about what you are creating.

I love to share the materials that I have been adding to my stitching tool kit. If you have been following along with me on social media, you have probably seen me adding new threads and supplies to my work. I will be going into detail about many of these new products that excite me in the embroidery world today.

If you are new to embroidery, do not let this chapter overwhelm you. Until you have fully embraced this craft, don't feel like you have to rush out and buy every single thread I mention or stock up on every bead out there! Find yourself the basic supplies and just start simply. Gradually experiment with specialty threads as you find what works for you. Add beads to your tool kit as you learn what your favorite stitches are. Start slowly.

SCISSORS

I use two pairs of scissors almost exclusively when I embroider. My Tula Pink large-ring 4" micro-tip scissors and my Fiskars Easy Action 5" micro-tip scissors.

The Tula Pink snips, besides being really shimmery and pretty to work with, have very sharp points. These tips work great for trimming threads, and the tiny points also allow you to work in small areas and make precise cuts while embroidering. Sometimes I need to trim something very close to the fabric and these are great for handling delicate cuts.

I do a lot of fussy cutting, and it would not be nearly as enjoyable if I did not have the micro-tip scissors. The spring-action handles allow for a good range of motion while cutting and do not strain your hand when you are making lots of precise cuts.

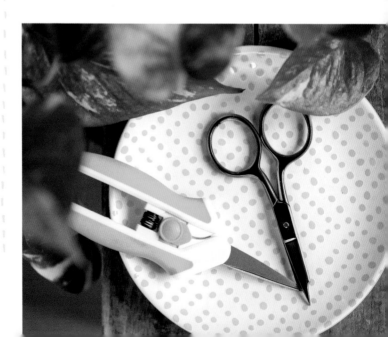

NEEDLES

My favorite type of needle is a milliners needle, and I have found that the Richard Hemming brand offers all the sizes I need, as well as other embroidery needles.

Milliners needles, which are also called straw needles, do not have a graduated shaft. The entire needle is the same thickness from top to bottom. These needles work great for embroidery and can also be used for beading.

Another plus is that milliners needles are quite inexpensive, so if you have trouble keeping track of them, it is not too much of a hit to the pocketbook every time you need to stock up on your supply.

THREAD

The threads that you use are so important to your embroidery. Much like paints to an artist, threads are the medium that you are creating with, so create a stash of thread that gets you excited to do some stitching.

All-Purpose Embroidery Thread

For almost every single project I stitch, my go-to thread is Eleganza Perle cotton. This Perle cotton collaboration from Sue Spargo and Wonderfil Specialty Threads comes on a spool in several different weights. With many embroidery threads, you have to divide the strands before use, but Eleganza thread does not need to be separated and can be stitched with 'as is' directly from the spool. It comes in three weights: the thickest weight is size 3, the medium weight is size 5, and the thinnest weight is a size 8. I know that is confusing, but remember that the sizing numbers go down as the weight increases, similar to the way larger beads are labeled with smaller numbers in the beading industry. When it comes to embroidery floss, I typically use sizes 5 and 8 in my work.

I love the Eleganza Perle cotton because of the way it stitches up with a slight sheen to it. If you look closely at the strand, you will notice a twist to the thread. When sewn onto a project, this thread layers beautifully and adds such a subtle texture to your piece.

Have I mentioned the colors? This brand offers an amazing array of colors! I have never not been able to find the color I wanted. This is also the reason that I have an embarrassingly large collection of this thread!

Beading Thread

When I first began incorporating beads into my embroidery, I was not picky about the thread I used. If it matched, I used it. Then I started using beads more often, and having the wrong thread really slowed me down. It's not fun to constantly stop stitching to untangle knots!

Then I discovered Sulky Petites. These are 12-weight threads, which is about the weight of two strands of embroidery floss. This thread also comes on spools and so doesn't need to be divided. The weight of this thread is perfect for both beading and stitching.

Sulky Petites thread also comes in a great variety of both solid and variegated colors. It even comes bundled in color packs, which makes color choosing easy if that is something you struggle with.

When I am beading, sometimes I like to hide the thread, but other times the thread is almost as much a part of the work as the beads are, so I really love the Sulky Petites for being functional but also being pretty to stitch with.

Silk Thread

The Thread Gatherer has a stunning array of hand-dyed silk threads that I love to use in my embroidery. For the past 25 years this small company has been creating threads that can be used for weaving and other needle arts.

Their silk threads are twelve-ply, which means you can use anywhere from one to twelve strands for embroidery. The choice is yours! I sometimes like a delicate line of stitching, so I will use four strands, but other times I will use all twelve for eye-catching impact. This is the best thread that I have found to use for the layers of the Victorian tufted stitch (see page 53).

Textural Threads

There are several other threads that I use in heavy rotation.

Rainbow Gallery sources some unique threads. My favorites are their Very Velvet and Fuzzy Stuff collections. The Very Velvet is just that, velvet thread. Made in Italy, it is a slightly thicker thread meant for needlepoint and cross-stitch, but works equally well with embroidery. Fuzzy Stuff is slightly finer than the Very Velvet and has an almost hairy appearance. It is a wonderful way to add wisps of texture to your embroidery.

Koigu Premium Merino (KPM) needlepoint yarn is made of 100% merino wool and has quickly become one of my top embroidery thread choices. Even though it is a thicker thread, it works great with the delicate and detailed demands of an embroidery project. Thicker threads can sometimes pose a challenge, especially when stitching through several layers, but I have never had trouble stitching with this particular type of yarn. The needlepoint yarn is a smaller skein than the regular skeins of KPM yarn, coming in at eleven yards, but is the exact same yarn. The smaller skein size allows you to have lots of colors in your stash of threads... maybe even all the colors!

The bold colors of Madeline Tosh's Unicorn Tails line caught my eye while I was browsing at my local yarn shop. I am always looking for a good neon to add to my stash and I found it among the skeins of Unicorn Tails. Made of merino wool from South Africa that has been hand-dyed in Texas, these are a fingering weight yarn that I have been using quite often in my embroidery. Of all yarn weights, fingering weight yarn, also called sock yarn, is one of the thinnest yarns available and one that typically works well in embroidery.

Last but not least on my list of favorite threads is Dala Perle cotton from Sue Spargo. The gorgeous array of colors, which all have fun names (always a bonus!), are hand-dyed by Kelly Spargo, Sue's daughter. They are dyed in small batches and are variegated with short repeats so you get lots of color variation in your stitches.

BEADS AND SEQUINS

One of my favorite ways to explore texture in embroidery is by adding seed beads and sequins to my projects. I have included several examples of combining embroidery with beads in the Boho floral samplers throughout Chapter 2. Seed beads come in a variety of materials and shapes, from circles and hexagons to glass and metal. The sizing works the same as it does in thread weights: the larger the number, the smaller the bead. For instance, a size 15 bead is much smaller than a size 3 bead. Using beads in your work is one of the easiest ways to get a lot of texture from a surprisingly small element.

If you are interested in adding beads to your embroidery stitches but aren't sure where to begin, check out the sample hoops that I have stitched up in Chapter Two. Another great source is CRK Design's Bead Embroidery Stitch Samples by Yasuko Endo, which has lots of pictures for inspiration.

WEAVING TOOLS

Weaving is a fun and unexpected way to add interesting bits and pieces to your embroidery, and I recommend three tools I think you will love.

The WEFTY Needle created by Tara Curtis is a tool designed to weave fabric strips. I tried to weave fabric strips before ever knowing this needle existed, and I never ended up with the neat and tight rows that this tool helps you to perfect! You can see a small example of my fabric weaving on the Quilt Barn hoop I created to go along with the pattern. My weaving is incredibly simple compared to the designs others have created with strips of fabric and a WEFTY Needle, but there's always room for improvement, right?

The Loome is another small weaving tool that will allow you to create anything from pom poms and tassels to cords and other small weavings. There are four models of the Loome available and with any of them, you can create a mini weaving project. The smallness of this tool allows you to slip it into a project bag with some spools of thread and carry it with you while on the go. I tend to practice my weaving skills while day-tripping in the car or waiting in the school pick-up line.

Kumihimo, Japanese braiding, is a cord weaving technique. Using a Kumihimo disk, you can create either a flat or tube-like cord with relative ease. There is a circle disk that creates a tubular cord and a square disk that creates one that is either a square or flat. You can get started with a simple pattern quickly and easily and then graduate to more complex patterns, even adding beads to the cord. I like using the cords to embroider details onto a project with the couching stitch. A great resource to check out is *Twist, Turn, & Tie 50 Japanese Kumihimo Braids* by Beth Kemp. I like that there are both simple and complex patterns within the pages of her book, so it is great for beginners or more advanced Kumihimo weavers.

CHAPTER 2

Exploring

TEXTURE

with Embroidery
Stitches

STITCHES USED

- **A** scalloped buttonhole chain stitch
- **B** oyster stitch
- **C** Spanish knotted feather stitch
- **D** bunched couching
- **E** woven spiderweb stitch
- **F** double lazy daisy
- **G** lattice stitch
- **H** woven filling stitch
- **I** eyelet stitch
- **J** shisha lattice stitch
- **K** colonial knots
- **L** knotted pearl stitch
- **M** cable plait stitch
- **N** wheatear stitch
- **O** Victorian tufted stitch

THE STITCHES

In the world of stitching, there is a vast array of stitches beyond the fifteen new ones included in this chapter. I chose them based on the lovely dimension that they can add to your projects. As I shifted my focus toward adding texture to my embroidery, I have found that these stitches are the ones I return to, time and again.

Several of the stitches in this chapter are based on simple foundation stitches that I demonstrated in *Boho Embroidery*, and I will note that in the instructions for the new stitch.

A fun challenge to give yourself is learning each of the fifteen stitches while embroidering on a fabric you love. For examples of this, I created the Boho Stitch Along (#bohosal) tag on social media. An ongoing, self-paced challenge, you choose a fabric, hoop it up, and begin to embroider. The beauty of this challenge is that there are no timelines, rules, or restrictions. You simply choose a fabric that appeals to you and you slowly begin the process of filling up that fabric with your stitches.

I created my own example of this in a large sampler hoop, using every one of the stitches you will learn here. By doing this, you are not only learning the stitches but by the end, you will have a beautiful embroidered sampler of your work to show for it. And even better: No two hoops will look the same!

The fabric in my large Boho sampler is by Amy Reber Designs. She created it for me to use specifically for this project. If you are interested in creating your own designs too, Spoonflower has developed a user-friendly website which walks you through the early steps to begin customizing fabric. If you aren't ready to make that jump, you can browse through their indie designer fabrics that are available for purchase.

On a smaller scale throughout this chapter, you will notice that I embroidered a separate Boho floral sampler for each stitch, using only one stitch per hoop. I love this because you can really see the beauty in limiting yourself to using a single stitch creatively in a project!

Now, let's get stitching!

PRACTICE HOOP

To reiterate a piece of advice I've mentioned before: I highly recommend working with a practice hoop alongside your project hoop. Having a practice hoop eliminates the fear of having less-than-perfect stitches in your finished project. You can practice each new stitch until you feel comfortable with moving on to your project hoop. I like to use fabric I enjoy looking at in my practice hoop, because it will be in my workspace and utilized a lot.

LET'S REVIEW

Here's a review of some essential stitches from *Boho Embroidery* to get you started:

SATIN STITCH

Satin stitching is used to fill an area, such as a petal on a flower or a geometric shape. Tip: For bigger areas, I find it helpful to place several stitches throughout my shape to use as guides. From there, you can continue to fill in the gaps with satin stitching. This technique helps you to keep your stitches even throughout the shape you are filling.

Bring the needle up at A and down at B. Continue until your shape is filled.

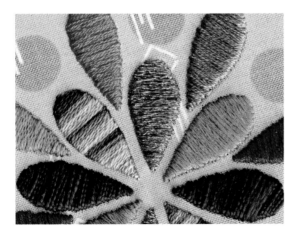

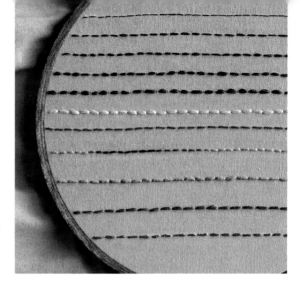

BACKSTITCH

The backstitch is a simple stitch that looks great as a border around the outside of your hoop. But it has just as much impact when you use it to highlight areas of fabric. Notice in the sampler that one or two strands of thread will make a delicate line, while four to six strands will make a bolder statement.

Bring the needle up at A and down at B. Continue until you want your line to end.

BOHO YOUR STITCHES! *Play with numbers! Use a combination of two-and four-strand stitches throughout your project. Work a circular border with six strands of thread around the inside of your hoop and then stitch a three-strand border parallel to that.*

RUNNING STITCH

It doesn't get any more basic than the running stitch, and yet, if you look at Sashiko designs, they look anything but basic. Sashiko, which means "little stabs," is a traditional form of Japanese embroidery that uses repeated running stitches to create patterns. Master this stitch and you are on your way to learning an entirely new form of embroidery. Or just master this stitch so that you can add nice straight stitching to your project. This stitch can be varied in length for a different look.

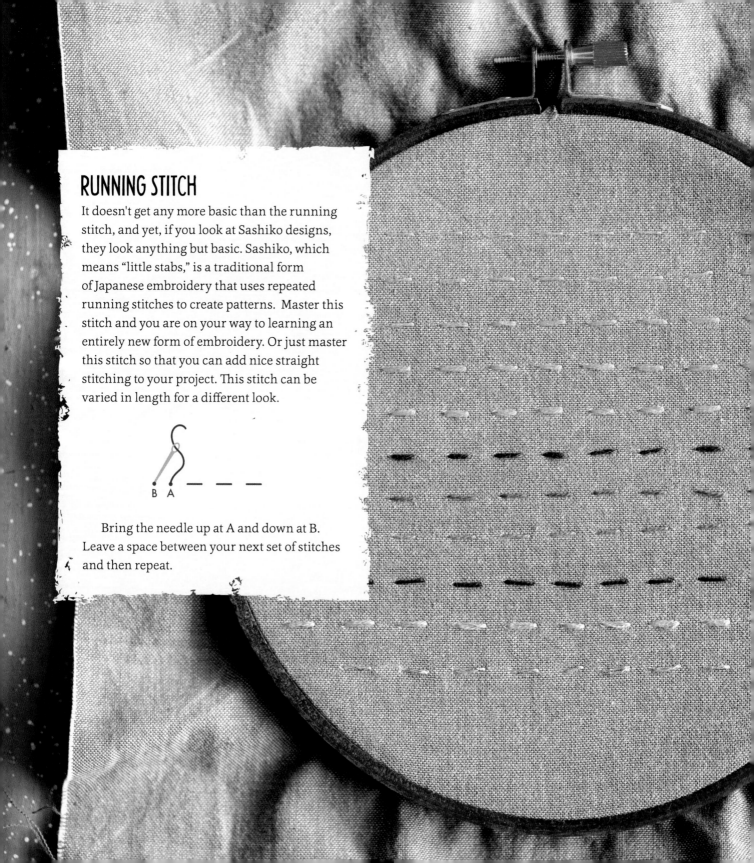

Bring the needle up at A and down at B. Leave a space between your next set of stitches and then repeat.

CHAIN STITCH

I love the braided appearance of the chain stitch. I relearned this stitch ages ago via instructions from Jenny Hart of *Sublime Stitching*. It completely changed how I felt about the chain stitch.

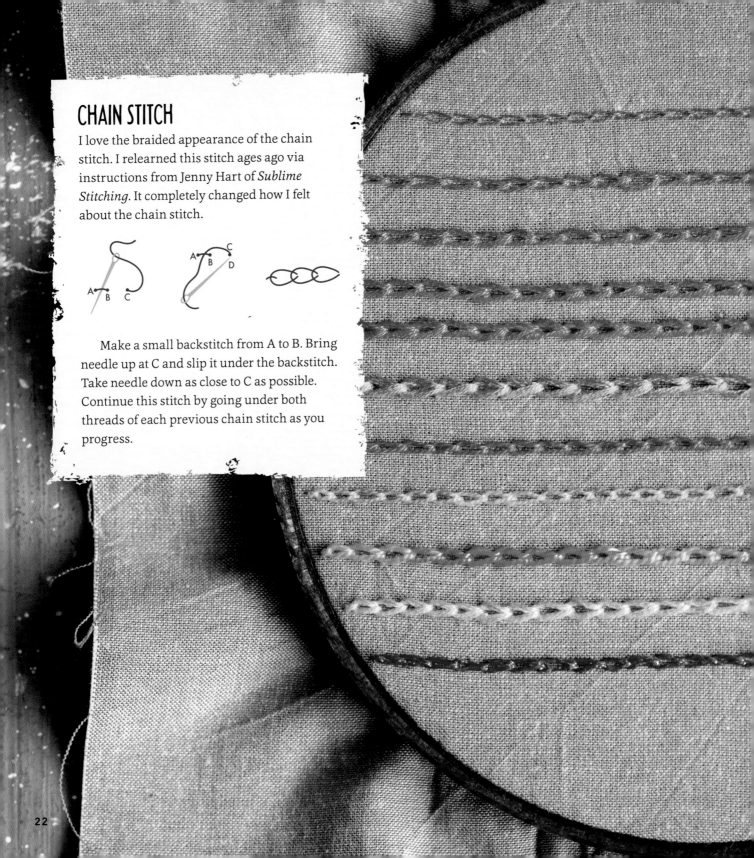

Make a small backstitch from A to B. Bring needle up at C and slip it under the backstitch. Take needle down as close to C as possible. Continue this stitch by going under both threads of each previous chain stitch as you progress.

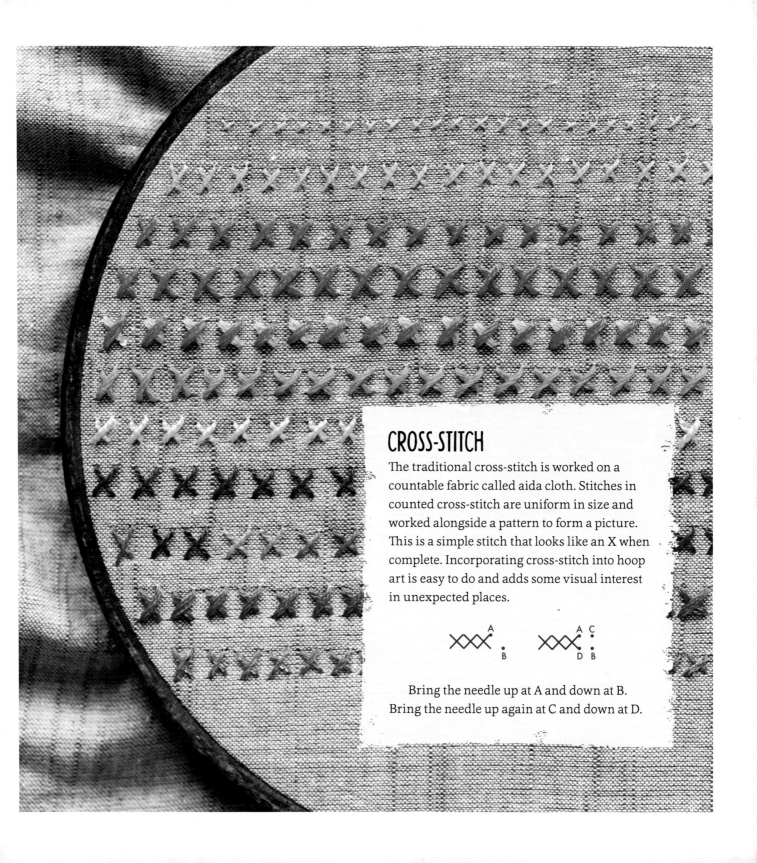

CROSS-STITCH

The traditional cross-stitch is worked on a countable fabric called aida cloth. Stitches in counted cross-stitch are uniform in size and worked alongside a pattern to form a picture. This is a simple stitch that looks like an X when complete. Incorporating cross-stitch into hoop art is easy to do and adds some visual interest in unexpected places.

Bring the needle up at A and down at B. Bring the needle up again at C and down at D.

KEEP IN MIND: *To create a consistently sized scallop, each chain in the chain stitch should be the same length. Pay attention to the tension of your thread. The first and last stitches of the scallop should be slightly tighter to achieve the scalloped look.*

BOHO YOUR STITCHES: *Chain stitch in a solid color and then work the buttonhole stitch in a contrasting color. Add beads in between each scallop. Use silk ribbon for a more substantial scalloped edge.*

TEXTURED STITCHES

SCALLOPED BUTTONHOLE CHAIN STITCH

This Boho floral mini sampler (opposite) has been stitched using fabric by Philip Jacobs for Free Spirit Fabrics.

The scalloped buttonhole chain stitch is a beautiful, decorative stitch that adds a scalloped border to your stitching. It is great for curves, ruffles, and edges.

Stitch a chain stitch foundation (see page 22). So, if you want to outline a leaf in this stitch, you will first chain stitch around the shape.

Next, begin the scallop. I work this stitch from the top to the bottom of the chain. Bring your needle and thread up at the point where you'd like the scallop to begin (A, below). From this point on, the rest of your stitches will be on top of the fabric.

Take your thread under the edge of the chain stitch that will have the scallop and over the thread that is currently in your needle (B). Pull the needle through.

Continue to the end of your chain stitch and then bring the needle and thread through to the back of your fabric and secure the loose ends.

SCANDALOUS STITCHES

Before I show you how this stitch is worked, I'm going to let you in on the controversy regarding the buttonhole stitch vs. the blanket stitch. They are actually different stitches that are inconsistently referred to as the same stitch on many occasions.

The difference is that the buttonhole stitch is worked with the needle stitching toward the *inside* of your project. Conversely, the blanket stitch is worked with the needle stitching toward the *outside* of your project. However, when worked, both of these stitches look similar and are used for similar finishes on the edge of a project. Adding to the confusion is the fact that these two stitches have been referred to and used interchangeably for many, many years.

For a complete and thorough reading of the buttonhole vs. blanket stitch debate, as well as other stitching-related topics, take a look at *Nordic Needle*.

Well, there's a load off of my mind. I can now teach you this stitch, knowing that you are well-informed about the controversy embedded in the name of the scalloped buttonhole chain stitch.

OYSTER STITCH

This Boho floral mini sampler (opposite) has been stitched using fabric by Amy Gibson for Windham Fabrics.

This stitch is great to use in places where you might typically use the satin stitch (see page 20). It looks swirly and decorative and can fill an area while adding dimension to your work.

BOHO YOUR STITCHES: By keeping the stitches tiny, they will stay compact and tightly coiled. By making the stitches longer, you will create stitches that look loose and wispy.

Bring the needle up through the fabric where you want the point of the oyster stitch to be placed (A, below).

To the left of that stitch, insert your needle (without taking the thread through) at (B) and bring the tip up at an angle to the right at (C). Pull the needle and thread through. (This will look like a single twisted chain stitch.)

Pass the needle through the thread at the point of the stitch at (D). Staying on top of the fabric, pass the needle and thread below the thread of the stitch.

Take the needle through the fabric at the spot where you just passed your thread at (E) but do not pull the thread completely through.

Bring your needle up at the edge of your new loop and secure it below the fabric at (F).

This stitch may feel slightly tedious at first and looks more complicated than it is. Once you get into the rhythm of stitching it, you will begin to enjoy the gentle woven loopiness of the oyster stitch!

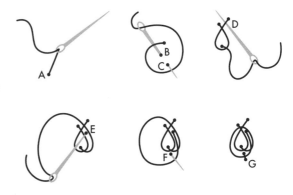

BOHO YOUR STITCHES: *Use a thicker thread or yarn, like a merino wool yarn. I love how this stitch looks like ric rack when stitched with a heavy thread! Try a shiny, silk thread or a thinner Perle cotton. See how different each material looks when stitched.*

SPANISH KNOTTED FEATHER STITCH

This Boho floral mini sampler (opposite) has been stitched using fabric by Bari J for Art Gallery Fabrics.

What I like most about the Spanish knotted feather stitch is the flexibility you have in working with it, both in narrow lines or in filling larger areas (like leaves). Depending on how you use this stitch, it takes on a completely different appearance.

I like to work from the right to the left. Bring your needle up through the fabric at (A, below). Then take your needle in at (B) slightly to the right and out of the fabric at an angle at (C) exiting above (A). Loop the thread over the needle again, then under the needle and pull the needle through the thread.

Your stitch will look like a small, off-center open chain stitch.

Take your needle down at (D) and up at an angle at (E). Wrap the thread over the needle, then under the needle again, and pull the needle through.

Continue. Each time you will bring your needle up into the middle of the twist in the stitch you just made and out at a diagonal.

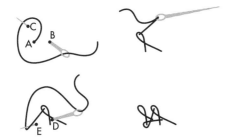

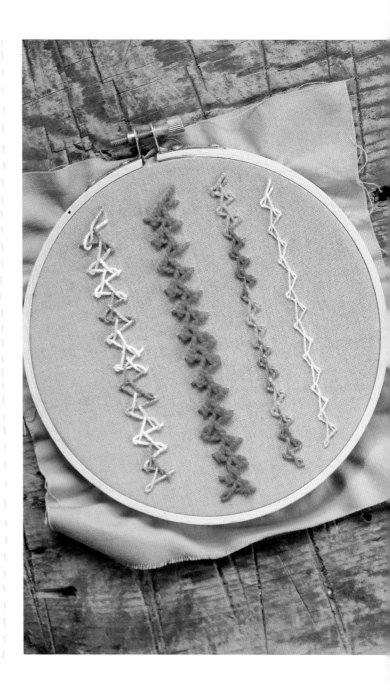

BUNCHED COUCHING

This Boho floral mini sampler (opposite) has been stitched using fabric by Heather Bailey for Free Spirit Fabrics.

This stitch is a slightly different version of the couching stitch that I taught in *Boho Embroidery*. I am showing you this one because using heavier weight fibers described in Chapter 1, creates a perfect "bunchiness."

BOHO YOUR STITCHES: *Use a combination of several threads to couch onto your fabric. You will get a great variety of texture and color with a very simple stitch! Use a yarn that you love but that is too thick to embroider with.*

Begin with a couching foundation stitch (the threads that are placed directly onto the fabric). If you know exactly how much thread you will need for this stitch, you can bring your thread up at the starting point at (A, below) and down at the end point at (B). Alternatively, you can bring your thread up at point at (A) and leave it on top of the fabric so that it can be moved around as you stitch (especially useful for curved lines of stitching shown in the photograph on the left).

With a second thread, you will be making straight stitches over the foundation thread to secure it to the fabric. You will find that you get the most puffiness when you bring your anchor thread in at (C) and then out at (D) very closely together under your foundation thread and then pull these stitches tight.

Continue adding C/D stitches at regularly spaced intervals until your foundation thread has been completely anchored to the fabric.

BOHO YOUR STITCHES: *As you are weaving your thread over and under, add a seed bead every so often to create even more visual interest in your stitches. This stitch is a great way to showcase a fancy variegated thread too.*

WOVEN SPIDERWEB STITCH

This Boho floral mini sampler (opposite) has been stitched using fabric by Katarina Roccella for Art Gallery Fabrics.

The woven spiderweb stitch is great for adding circles of raised texture to your work. It also works well for creating circles for floral details.

However, I feel like I need to add a disclaimer: This stitch is a major thread eater. Did you ever say to yourself, "I just have so much thread ... I wish I knew of a single stitch that would help me unload all of this extra thread!" Well, look no further than the woven spiderweb stitch! Despite that one drawback, this is a really beautiful stitch and a way to practice thread weaving in a small area.

Begin with an odd number of straight stitches. Bring your needle up at (A, below), down at the center, up at (B), down at the center, and continue until you have an odd number of foundation stitches in the shape of an asterisk.

Bring your weaving thread up near the center (A) and begin weaving your thread over (B) and under (C). Continue all the way around in a circle until your foundation stitches have been completely covered.

DOUBLE LAZY DAISY STITCH

This Boho floral mini sampler (opposite) has been stitched using fabric by Laundry Basket Quilts for Moda Fabrics.

A simple, but beautiful, way to add highlighting and shading to your work is the double lazy daisy stitch. It is a stitch that brings subtle texture to your work without over-complicating it. If you can do the chain stitch and a lazy daisy, then you have already mastered the double lazy daisy!

BOHO YOUR STITCHES: *Use one color for your inside lazy daisy but vary the outside thread color to add highlights throughout the piece. Use a thin thread for the inside lazy daisy and a thicker thread for the outside flower. Why stop at just a double lazy daisy? Be adventurous and add an occasional triple lazy daisy into the mix!*

Begin with the center, or the smaller, lazy daisy stitch first. Bring your needle and thread up at (A, below), pull through, and then take your needle down at (A), but this time do not pull your thread completely through.

Secure this stitch by bringing your needle up at (B) and then down at (C), going over your daisy petal.

For your next stitch, bring your needle up at (D), pull the thread through, and then take the needle down again at (D), not pulling the thread completely through as you did for the first lazy daisy.

Secure that second petal by bringing your needle up at (E) and then down at (F), pulling the thread completely through.

BOHO YOUR STITCHES: *You are not limited to how you anchor your threads to the fabric! Vary by using small cross stitches, star shapes, multiple thread colors, etc. Stitch a foundation of satin stitches and then add your lattice stitches on top for some great raised texture!*

LATTICE STITCH

This Boho floral mini sampler (opposite) has been stitched using fabric by Kaffe Fassett for Rowan Fabrics.

The lattice stitch is a versatile stitch to use in place of a filling stitch, such as the satin stitch (see page 20). It fills an area with texture, and by varying the threads used, it can look like a heavier stitch, one that is airier. There are many options with this stitch!

Begin with your foundation stitches, bringing your needle up at (A, below), down at (B) and repeat until you have vertically filled your area to be stitched.

This is considered 'laid work', because your next rows of stitches are laid directly on top of your vertical foundation stitches. Bring your needle and thread up at (C) and down at (D).

Next, secure the threads to the fabric. Bring your needle up at (F) and diagonally down at (G). You are making a small stitch where both foundation stitches meet.

Continue until all of your threads have been secured to the fabric.

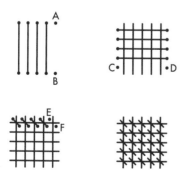

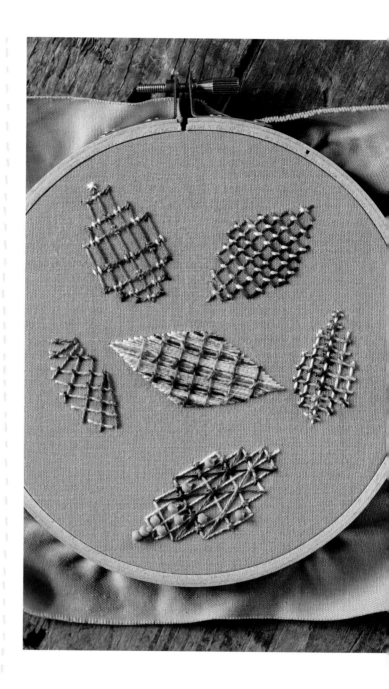

WOVEN FILLING STITCH

This Boho floral mini sampler (opposite) has been stitched using fabric by Jennifer Paganelli for Free Spirit Fabrics.

If you are looking for a filling stitch to cover larger areas with texture, the woven filling stitch is for you. You are not limited to working in just a square shape. This stitch can fill petals, leaves, or even small accent areas in your embroidery.

> **BOHO YOUR STITCHES**: *Try using thick threads as the foundation stitches and thinner threads to weave. Use a metallic thread to weave between your foundation stitches.*

Begin this stitch the same way you begin the lattice stitch (see page 37). Stitch a section of foundation stitches bringing your thread up at (A, below) and down at (B).

Choose your weaving thread. I like to start in the middle section of my work to keep my stitches nicely lined up. You may want to start at the top and work toward the bottom (experiment to see which way works best for you). Bring your thread up at (C), and from here weave over and under your foundation stitches. Bring your needle and thread down at (D).

Continue until you have finished your weaving.

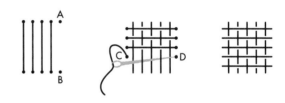

BOHO YOUR STITCHES: *Change the appearance of your eyelets by varying the size of the holes you punch with the awl. Try stitching both larger and smaller eyelets. Use a thick thread around the edges to make an edge that stands out from the fabric.*

EYELET STITCH

This Boho floral mini sampler (opposite) has been stitched using fabric by Anna Maria Horner for Free Spirit Fabrics.

Whenever I see eyelets worked into fabric, I am reminded of sweet dresses for little ones or delicate linens that are worn from use over time. I just love the look of eyelets! They can be a fun and unexpected addition to embroidery.

USING AN AWL

You will need a tailor's awl in addition to your regular embroidery kit to create an eyelet. I have tried to stitch eyelets both with and without a tailor's awl, and the results are always nicer when you begin with a hole punched from an awl rather than a hole cut with scissors.

Using an awl, punch a hole where you want your eyelet to be (A, below). Work the hole open by sliding the awl in and out. If you need to make the opening slightly bigger, cut away the tiny edges with a pair of sharp scissors.

Bring the needle up at (B) and pull the thread through.

Position your needle back down in the center hole (C) pulling your thread through and coming back up at (D).

Continue this all the way around the circle of the eyelet until the raw edges are secured with thread.

KEEP IN MIND: *I have found that the eyelet stitch is easier to achieve when the fabric is not pulled super taut in the hoop. For this one, you want a little bit of give in the fabric as you are stitching.*

SHISHA LATTICE STITCH

This Boho floral mini sampler (opposite) has been stitched using fabric by Rebecca Bischoff for Robert Kaufman Fabrics. The buttons were made using fabric from Leslie Tucker Jenison for RJR Fabrics.

There are several variations on the shisha stitch, and all of them allow you to add a mirror or button or flat disc to your embroidery. To see other variations of this stitch, I recommend Mary Corbet's Needle 'n Thread (needlenthread.com), which has excellent video tutorials that will walk you through some of the more complicated versions.

I love the shisha lattice stitch! Using it will enable you to quickly and simply add a three-dimensional object to your embroidery.

Choose your object and place it on the fabric.

This will work up just like the woven filling stitch (see page 33). Bring your needle and thread up at (A, below), down at (B), up at (C), down at (D). Repeat until stitches cover the surface of your object. The number of stitches used will vary depending on your object.

Begin the thread weaving by bringing the needle and thread up at (E), weave over and under the threads and then take your needle and thread down at (F). Continue, beginning at (G), weaving over and under the threads and ending at (H). Repeat until the object is secured.

Finish by adding a chain stitch (see page 22) border around the object.

BOHO YOUR OBJECTS:

Cover fabric buttons with coordinating or contrasting fabrics and add them to your embroidery. Add a decorative vintage button. Always be on the lookout for interesting flat objects that can be easily added to your embroidery projects!

BOHO YOUR STITCHES:
Colonial knots are great for securing sequins to your fabric! Thread a sequin and place it flat on your fabric. Then tie your colonial knot. The knot will be large enough to keep the sequin in place!

COLONIAL KNOTS

This Boho floral mini sampler (opposite) has been stitched using fabric by Martha Negley for Westminster Fibers.

Colonial knots are the main stitch used in a type of embroidery called candlewick embroidery. Also known as candlewicking, this embroidery is typically done with white thread on a white (usually muslin) fabric. This type of embroidery was created by women who desired to do handwork but also needed to conserve fabrics and threads because they were a precious commodity at the time this method was popular. They embroidered with a very thick type of thread that was also used to make the wick of candles. As a result, the finished knots made a beautiful raised pattern. If you are interested in learning more about the history of this embroidery stitch, Nordic Needle has a fascinating article on how candlewick embroidery first came about.

Colonial knots are a nice alternative to French knots and can be used anywhere that you would use a French knot. They are my preferred method for knotting because I like the way they appear slightly larger and loopier than French knots.

> **KEEP IN MIND**: *The key to this stitch is keeping a consistent tension on your thread throughout the stitching.*

Bring your needle and thread up through the fabric where you want your first knot to be at (A, below). Hold the thread so that it looks like a backward letter C and place the needle in the middle of the C shape.

The needle remains where it is while you twist the thread up and over the needle and then below the needle. Your thread will look like the number 8.

Keeping the tension of the thread, insert the needle next to where you came up at (B) and pull the needle and thread below the fabric, making your first colonial knot.

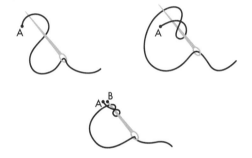

KNOTTED PEARL STITCH

This Boho floral mini sampler (opposite) has been stitched using fabric by Amy Butler for Rowan/Westminster Fibers.

The knotted pearl stitch is one of my favorite stitches. It is such an easy stitch and is incredibly versatile. It can easily be worked on curves or lines for borders. It looks eye-catching if you use thicker thread.

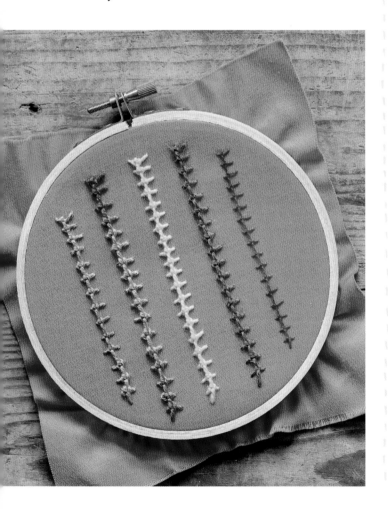

Work this stitch from right to left. Begin with a small foundation stitch, coming up at (A, below) and going down at (B).

Bring your needle and thread up at (C) and go under the (A–B) foundation stitch.

Once your needle is under the stitch, bring your working thread under the needle and pull it through. You just created a small knot.

Slide your needle under the stitch/knot that you just created, as well as under your working thread and pull through, creating a second knot.

To continue, bring your needle and thread down at (D). Come up at (E).

Bring your needle under the diagonal stitch you just created and under your thread to make the knot (as before). Repeat to create your second knot and continue working along your fabric.

You will end up with a neat row of knotted stitches.

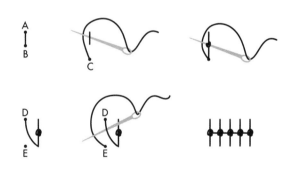

KEEP iN MiND: *The great thing about this stitch is that if you feel your knots are off center, you can gently move their position with your needle until you are happy with how they are spaced.*

CABLE PLAIT STITCH

This Boho floral mini sampler (opposite) has been stitched using fabric by Amy Butler for Free Spirit Fabrics.

The cable plait stitch, also known as the braid stitch, works well on borders and curves and has a thick look when finished. Once you get into the stitching groove with this, it stitches up quickly and it is fun to see the braid develop as you go.

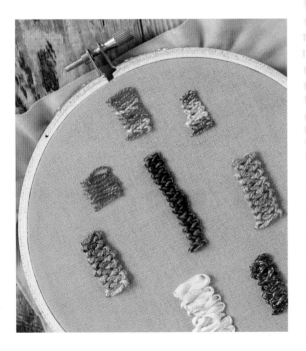

Work this stitch from top to bottom.

Bring your needle and thread up at (A, below) and wrap your thread over and under your needle.

Keep the tension on the wrapped thread and insert your needle at (B).

While still holding the thread, bring your needle up at (C).

Take the needle in front of the working thread and pull through. You just made your first stitch.

Continue and you will get a thick braided line of stitching.

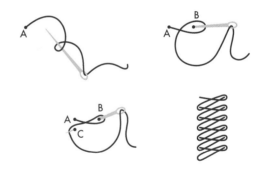

WHEATEAR STITCH

This Boho floral mini sampler (opposite) has been stitched using fabric by Anna Maria Horner for Free Spirit Fabrics.

You gotta love a stitch that is so versatile that it can be stitched together to form a line or it can be stitched separately to form individual, stand-alone stitches. The wheatear stitch is one of those flexible stitches that works well on curves and borders as well as in accent areas.

While stitching this, you may be reminded of the chain stitch (see page 22) because it does stitch up into a nice chain with the added bonus of accent lines at the top of each new stitch.

BOHO YOUR STITCHES: *Add a sequin or seed bead to the chain part of the wheatear stitch as you are embroidering and bring this stitch to the next level of Boho-ness!*

Begin with a small stitch, bringing your needle and thread up at (A) and down at (C). Your next stitch will come up at (B) and also down at (C).

Bring your thread up at (D) and slide it beneath the V that you just formed, bringing the needle and thread back down at (D). You just formed a single wheatear stitch.

To continue and make a chain, bring your thread up at (E), down at (F), which is where your previous stitch ended, up at (G), and down at (F).

Continue as before and you will soon have a row of wheatear stitches.

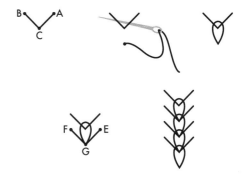

BOHO YOUR STITCHES: *Use a different color for each layer and the end result will be a lovely blend of colors.*

VICTORIAN TUFTED STITCH

This Boho floral mini sampler (opposite) has been stitched using fabric by Amy Reber for Free Spirit Fabrics.

The Victorian tufted stitch will impress you with its fluffiness and ease.

If you learned the herringbone stitch from Boho Embroidery, then you already know how to do this stitch. But now let's add a twist.

Begin with a row of closed herringbone stitches. This row will be the narrowest layer of the tufted stitch and is the base layer, so it needs to be a nice, thick layer of stitches.

When your first row is complete, stitch another row of closed herringbone stitches directly over the top. I like to start slightly before my previous first stitch and end slightly after my previous last stitch.

Your last row of stitches will be a third row of herringbone stitches that are made directly on top of your two previous rows.

Now for the fun part! Take a sharp micro-tip pair of scissors and cut down the middle of your rows of stitches, taking care to snip each layer.

Using either a clean eyebrow brush or a bunka brush (a small fingertip wire brush specifically meant for this job), fluff the threads to make them soft and full. Trim carefully if you want to change the shape or height of your stitches and fluff some more until you are happy with the shape and fluffiness!

CHAPTER 3

PATTERN TRANSFER
Techniques

Every pattern in this book has been designed to be used in three different ways: 1) as a standard embroidery pattern, 2) as a fabric appliqué pattern, and 3) as a combination of both methods: embroidery and appliqué.

When choosing a background fabric to transfer your pattern onto, the size of your hoop (or canvas) will determine how much fabric you will need. I rarely measure my fabrics, but instead will place the hoop that I plan to use on top of the fabric and cut around it, leaving approximately 2" of excess at the edge.

Once you have decided which fabric and pattern you want to begin with, the next question is: "How do I get my pattern onto the fabric"

In this chapter I will share my favorite methods for dissecting an embroidery pattern and transferring patterns from paper to fabric.

EMBROIDERY PATTERN & TRANSFER PENS

Gather your materials: a photocopy or print out of the pattern, fabric to transfer your pattern onto, scissors, an embroidery hoop, a light source (a light box or access to a window), and a fabric pen. I prefer to use either a Sulky iron-on transfer pen or a Dritz Mark-B-Gone marking pen.

SULKY IRON-ON TRANSFER PEN

The Sulky iron-on transfer pen is used directly on the pattern paper. Look at the pattern and decide which way you want it to transfer onto your fabric. For example, if you want your finished piece to look like the hoop in the book, trace the pattern onto the back side of the paper. If you want your pattern to mirror what you see in the book, trace directly on top of the lines on the pattern.

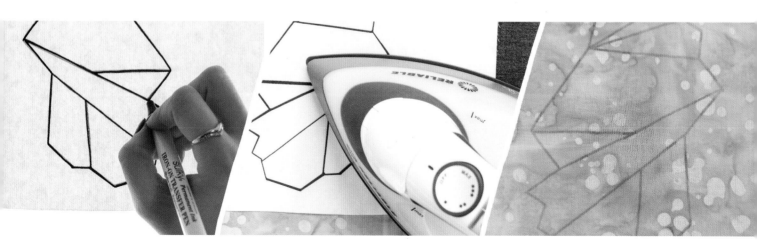

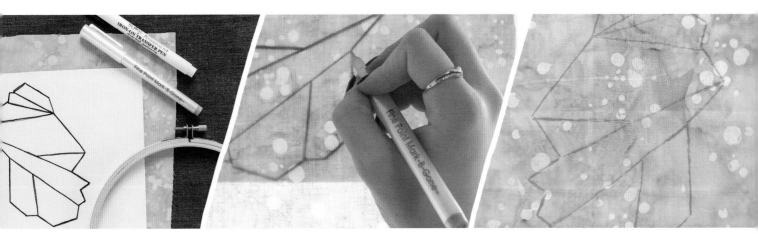

Once you have traced the entire pattern, place the side with the transfer pen marks on the right side of the fabric. Following the directions on the pen packaging, iron the pattern directly onto your fabric.

NOTE: *The marks from the Sulky iron-on transfer pen are permanent, so be sure to position the pattern correctly on the fabric before ironing. Once the image is transferred, it is there to stay!*

Your pattern is now ready to add embroidery!

DRITZ MARK-B-GONE MARKING PEN

The Dritz Mark-B-Gone marking pen is used directly on the right side of the fabric. Place the print out or photocopy of the pattern on a light source (like a sunny window or a light box), paying close attention to the direction of your choosing. Position the fabric directly on top of the pattern with the wrong side facing the light source. Trace the pattern onto the fabric.

Your pattern is now ready to add embroidery!

NOTE: *The marks from the Dritz Mark-B Gone marking pen dissolve with water. If you change your mind, you can rinse the fabric, let it dry, and then begin the transfer process again.*

FABRIC APPLIQUÉ PATTERN

This method will seem familiar to you if you have already read Boho Embroidery. It is one of my favorite time-tested methods for creating an embroidery project!

It helps to look at an embroidery pattern and mentally dissect it before cutting into your fabric. Almost anything can be turned into an embroidery pattern. With a little patience, this method will help you do just that with not only the patterns from this book but also patterns that you may create on your own.

Gather your materials: a photocopy or print out of the pattern, fusible interfacing (I like HeatnBond Lite), scissors, a variety of fabrics, an embroidery hoop, a light source (a light box or access to a window), and a fabric pen. See page 56 for information on my favorite fabric pens.

Choose a background fabric and cut a square that will fit nicely in your hoop, then set it aside. Cut a square of fusible interfacing the same size. Place the pattern right side down on a light source, and trace it onto the interfacing.

> **TIP**: *If your pattern has pieces that sit on top of one another, first trace all of the outer pieces. If the pattern has inside pieces, shift the interfacing to an unused section and trace those pieces as well, until all the pieces have been transferred onto the interfacing. Leave at least ¼" between the shapes for cutting.*

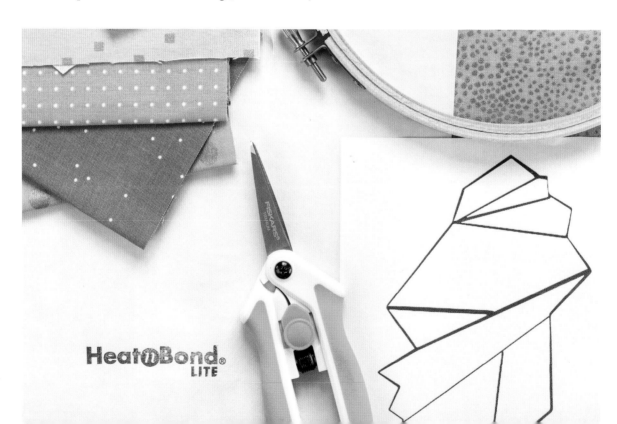

Once all of the pieces have been traced, roughly cut out the pattern pieces from the interfacing. Do not trim the pieces too closely to the pattern shapes just yet.

Gather a selection of fabrics to use with the pattern. One by one, place the fusible interfacing pieces onto the wrong side of your chosen fabric and iron them in place following the directions on the packaging.

TIP: *It helps to remember that the shiny side of the fusible interfacing is always placed facedown on the fabric. Never place an iron directly on top of the shiny side of the interfacing or the adhesive will transfer to the iron and create a burning, gummy mess. Place an iron only on the paper side of the interfacing.*

Allow the pattern piece to cool for a few seconds, then finely cut out the shapes from the fabric.

When each pattern piece is cut from the fabric, peel off the paper backing from each one and arrange the pieces on your background fabric square. Depending on the complexity of the pattern, it may be best to iron the pieces down one at a time to minimize shift. This process takes patience, but when you have finished, you are ready to hoop up and embroider your piece!

REMEMBER! *Use the pattern as a guide, knowing that there is leeway in arranging the pieces. For example, if you look very closely at my stitched Hydrangea pattern in Chapter 6, you will see that the flowers are in a slightly different position from that shown on the pattern. If you are happy with how the transferred pattern pieces look as a collage, then that is all that matters!*

EMBROIDERY PATTERN & TRANSFER SHEETS

Do you love the idea of working with one of these patterns as strictly embroidery, but want an even more precise method of transferring a pattern?

If you have access to a computer/scanner/copier, consider using Sulky Stick 'n Stitch printable sheets. I absolutely love the ease of working with these sheets! The sheets are 8½" x 11" and typically come in packs of twelve.

Gather your materials: the pattern, a Stick 'n Stitch printable sheet, fabric, scissors, and an embroidery hoop.

Following the directions on the transfer sheets, print or photocopy the pattern directly onto a Stick 'n Stitch sheet.

Trim around the design, leaving an approximately ½" border around the outside of the shape.

Peel the paper backing off and firmly press the design onto the right side of the fabric with your hands. You can also baste around the edges to keep the paper adhered to the fabric and to minimize any shifting between the pattern and fabric.

Your pattern is now ready to add your embroidery! You will embroider directly onto the design and paper. When you have finished, follow the package directions for rinsing the project in water and washing the adhesive paper away or simply remove the basting stitches.

EMBROIDERY & FABRIC APPLIQUÉ COMBO PATTERN

This method is a combination of the standard transfer methods and the fabric appliqué methods.

First, transfer your pattern onto the background fabric using the standard embroidery transfer method of your choice (see page 56).

Choose elements of the same pattern that you want to incorporate as appliqué. Trace those elements on fusible interfacing (as instructed on page 58), paying close attention to the orientation of the pieces within the pattern.

Iron the pieces in place within the pattern on the background fabric. You are now ready to begin embroidering!

THE FINISHING PROCESS

When you have finished stitching, pull the fabric taut, making sure there are no wrinkles in the fabric, then tighten the hoop screw one last time. Trim the fabric around the hoop, leaving approximately ½". Using washable white glue, run a strip onto the wood hoop on the back side of the project. Fold the fabric over the edge of the hoop and allow to dry before displaying. Consider covering the back of the hoop with a piece of felt to hide the back of your stitches. Insert the felt into the back of the hoop. The felt will stay in place and can be easily removed whenever you want to see the back of your work!

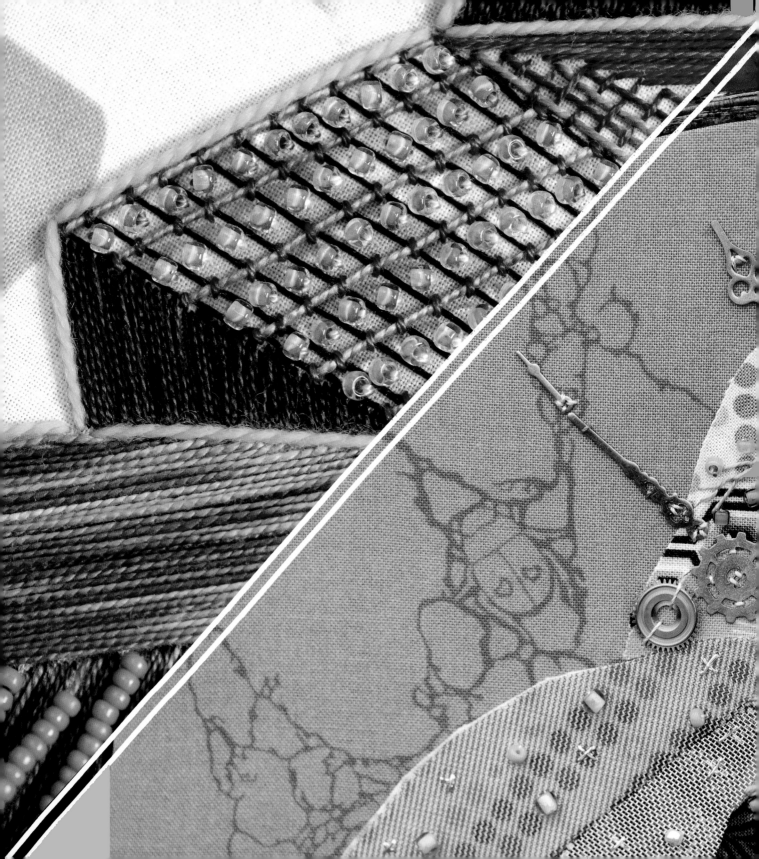

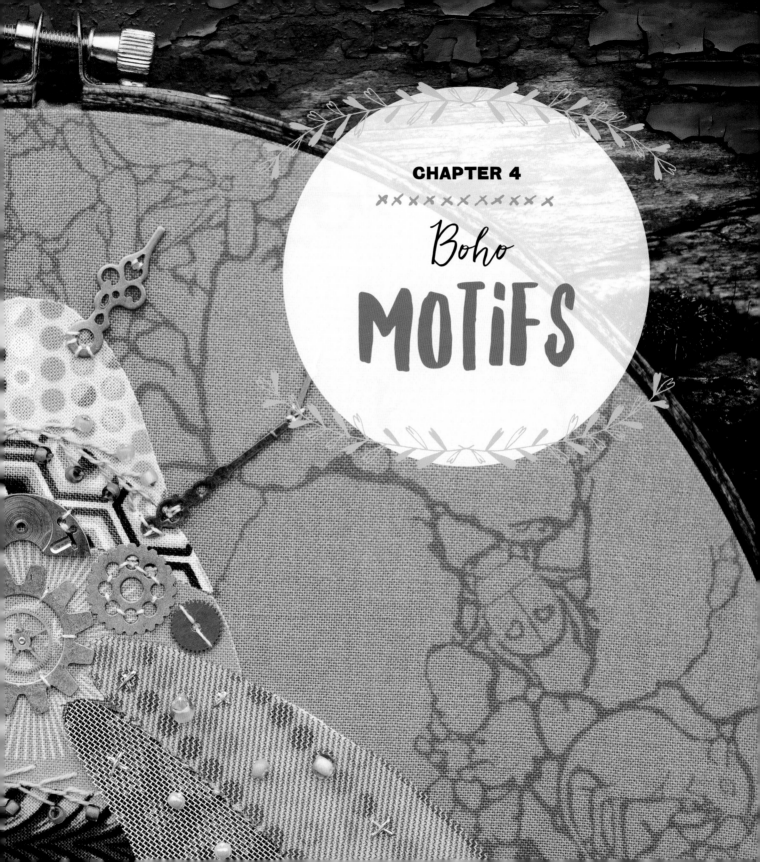

CHAPTER 4

x x x x x x x x x x

Boho

MOTIFS

PATTERNS INSPIRED BY COLOR

Each pattern I created for this book was designed to be stitched as a regular embroidery or an appliqué pattern. The patterns can also be used as color inspiration pages. Photocopy the pages and add color to help you determine the palette you want to work with.

As you decide on fabrics for your projects, give special consideration not only to the feature fabrics but also to the background fabric. If you really want to embrace the freedom that comes with Boho embroidery, try choosing a fabric that complements the theme of your pattern and allows you to add stitches and embellishments to that. So much of what I enjoy about embroidery comes from looking to the fabrics themselves as inspiration. You'll notice that many of my stitched-up patterns focus on the background fabric just as much as the main embroidery pattern.

If you follow my stitching journey on Instagram (@wildboho), or if you've flipped through the pages of this book, it will come as no surprise to you that I love working with color. The more saturated my colors are, the better! To challenge myself and expand my stitching palette, I sometimes work on a project that limits my use of color to something more neutral and subdued.

However, none of the project examples in this section are neutral and subdued! I encourage you to have fun creating your own saturated palette of fabrics and threads as you delve into each of these designs. The simple lines allow your color, thread and stitch choices to shine in your finished piece.

If working with color seems overwhelming and you're not sure where to even begin, I highly recommend looking through a book that explores color in detail. One of my favorites is *Color Inspirations* by Darius A. Monsef IV. This book is filled with small circles, each one a different color palette. I like how the book is broken into sections by main color, so if you have a focus color in mind, you can turn to that section and see a variety of combinations that might work for your project. I find myself leafing through this book when I'm not sure what color direction to take in a project, and I always settle on something new and exciting!

ARE YOU ON PINTEREST? *Create a color inspiration board for yourself with color palettes that inspire you. Keep adding to your board, and when you find yourself unsure of color choices, look through your pictures that contain combinations you already know you like!*

Don't be afraid of color. When you begin a project from this chapter, I encourage you to step out of your color comfort zone and try something new!

ARCHITECTURE INSPIRATION

I love barns. Living in Bucks County, Pennsylvania, I have all around me gorgeous barns, some well-preserved and some well-weathered. No matter the state of the building, I find that there is such simple beauty in the architecture of a barn.

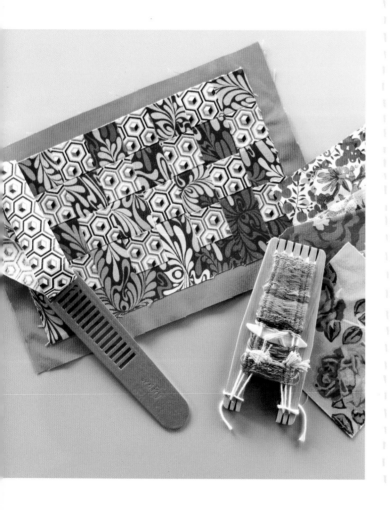

When I created this pattern, I had in mind photographs of a brightly colored quilt held up against the backdrop of a barn. But I also pictured barns in the western part of the United States, where quilts have been painted near the tops of the buildings. This is a form of art that I would love to see embraced on the barns in our area. But, until that happens, with this pattern, I can have my very own mini barn quilt all hooped up!

I kept the barn in this pattern simple because the idea is to create a lovely mini quilt in the rectangle area that is left blank near the roof. This could be created with a pattern of embroidery stitches or it could be an actual teeny-tiny quilt.

My barn quilt was created using thin fabric strips that I cut and then wove together with my WEFTY Needle, forming a small quilt just perfect for hanging on a miniature barn!

You might choose to make your barn quilt with a small yarn weaving, like the ones that I made with the Loome weaving tool pictured in the photo on the left, or you may want to use a beautiful scrap of fabric that you love to look at.

And speaking of beautiful fabrics, the background fabric that I chose for this pattern is a boldly colored floral that allowed me to add decorative stitches both on the barn itself and on the background. I like to think that this barn is settled into a field of wildflowers! Have fun with your background fabric on this project.

STAINED GLASS INSPIRATION

The next three patterns were inspired by my love of stained glass works of art. On nearly every window in my house, I have a colorful piece of stained glass that beautifully reflects the light that shines through it. Looking at stained glass just makes me happy. Some are vintage pieces I have picked up at thrift stores and yard sales, and some are new pieces that hold the memories of places I have visited. In the cold and dark days of winter, these colorful artworks remind me of the colorful, warmer days that are ahead!

STAINED GLASS PINEAPPLE

The pineapple is a widely recognized symbol of hospitality that can be found in home decor, from modern to bohemian, elegant to eclectic.

For this pattern, I wanted to take something familiar and make it slightly unexpected by breaking it up and dividing it into sections of color.

You can enlarge this pattern and use the fabric appliqué method to add your favorite pieces of fabric to it. Or you can use only one stitch in a variety of textures and colors, as I did with this hoop, stitching it entirely in the satin stitch.

There are two versions of this pattern. One is blank except for the design and the other is marked with letters that will help you to choose your colors.

STAINED GLASS CHOPPY WATERS

This pattern came from my love of the ocean. Every time I make my way to the Jersey shore, the water is a different shade of blue, sometimes angry and gray, sometimes calm and reminiscent of the Caribbean. This pattern challenges you to work within a monochromatic color palette. I picture it being stitched in every shade of blue!

My hoop is stitched all in blues. Because the design is more open, your background fabric choice is very visible and adds to the design of your hoop. I chose a brightly colored fabric with a nautical feeling for my hoop. For lots of added texture, I used a combination of Perle cotton, Fuzzy Stuff and Very Velvet threads.

STAINED GLASS TRANQUIL FIELDS

With a versatile color palette, the tranquil fields pattern can span the seasons. From winter fields stitched in a palette of white, to spring and summer fields in hues of green, and autumn fields in golds. I love patterns that can be stitched several times over and look different every time!

For my hoop, I envisioned patchwork fields, and I achieved that look with the fabric appliqué method of embroidery. While this method may take more time, cutting out and ironing so many small pieces is worth your while.

If you are a fabric scrap collector, this is the perfect project for you. I kept the thread colors simple, using just black and gray because there were so many colors in the fabrics themselves.

TEXTURED INSPIRATION

Evoking memories of summertime mornings with hot air balloons passing slowly over my house, this pattern can handle all the texture you are willing to add to it: from fur to tulle, velvet, or lace. You can even work with quilting cottons in a variety of patterns: floral, plaid, or stripes. I love patterns that do not require large amounts of fabric, because I feel as if I can be more adventurous with scraps of texture.

In my example, I chose to use bold fabrics combined with simple stitches. Neon faux fur, wool, lightweight gauzy fabrics and quilting cottons combined to create a beautifully colored palette, with some of my favorite hues.

TEST YOUR FABRICS! *Always test the fabrics you want to use to see how they do with the fusible interfacing before you begin your project. I have found that heavier fabrics like wool and fur adhere differently than sheer fabrics. Do a test with a small piece of fabric so you don't ruin your precious scraps!*

As with any embroidery pattern, you can isolate one section to change the focal point and add variety. I chose to create an additional hoop that isolates one hot air balloon from the pattern.

GO BOHO WITH YOUR FABRIC CHOICES!

This is your opportunity to mix up your fabrics and play with textures. Use scraps of silk or velvet. Rummage through small bits of ribbon and lace you have hoarded. In thrift shops, look for clothes with interesting textures that you can cut up to repurpose as fabric.

PATTERNS INSPIRED BY SHAPE

As a stitcher, I find it to be so satisfying to fill shapes within fabric designs and embroidery motifs with additional color. That color can come from thread, beads or fabric. To watch the shape become a piece of art that I have personalized through each of my choices, is such a thrill.

When I am creating my own embroidered versions of these patterns, it feels like I am disassembling the pattern and then reassembling all of the fabric pieces that make up an intricate puzzle. For the Gemstone Cluster pattern, for instance, taking all of the pieces I have cut out and then reassembled to create the design feels like an accomplishment! Challenge yourself by diving into one of these shape-based patterns and feel that same excitement as you transform shapes into a completed piece with your stitches, fabrics, and embellishments.

SUN (OR MOON) AND THE MOUNTAINS

Boho embroidery is all about forging ahead with your own unique stitching style, and what better way to do that than with a pattern that can be adapted to suit your personal style and preferences?

With the Sun (or Moon) and Mountains pattern, you can take one of two different paths to create your own hoop. Do you want to create a hoop that is the daytime or nighttime version of this pattern? You can see in my sample hoops, my daytime version features a golden sun and mountains in shades of greens and browns. For my nighttime version, I simply changed the color palette. You can see a silvery moon and mountains in shades of purples and blues.

Looking to customize this pattern even more? After adding your mountains, freestyle stitch your own trees in the foreground! Can you imagine yourself living in tranquility here? Then create a small house and stitch that as well. I love patterns that lend themselves to such variety!

GEMSTONES AND GEODES

The following three gemstone and geode patterns can be stitched as a trio, or you can choose to stitch just one to add some natural geometric shapes to your decor.

The flat Geodes pattern will allow you the most flexibility as you can see from my stitched-up version on canvas. The canvas contains all four geodes from the pattern with their positions slightly altered. You can pick and choose your own geodes to stitch. By isolating just one in a hoop and placing it in a different direction — like I did by positioning the geode shape horizontally in an oval hoop — you will end up with a unique geode project that takes on a brand-new look.

For the Gemstone Cluster hoop, which I created using the fabric appliqué method, I enlarged the pattern 135%. This is a great example that shows you how enlarging a pattern makes the fabric appliqué process slightly easier, especially if this is your first time experimenting with it. The larger fabric pieces also allow more of the patterns from the fabric to show in your finished piece.

I stitched the Geometric Gemstone as a standard embroidery pattern to showcase several of the more decorative filling stitches, such as the lattice stitch and the woven filling stitch. Using beads with my embroidery gives a bit of sparkle to what is naturally a glittery object!

TRY KUMIHIMO! *A fun way to add texture to the Geodes pattern is by making Kumihimo braids and then using the couching stitch to adhere them to the lines on your pattern. This Japanese braiding technique uses a foam board that allows the threads to be woven together to form a pattern. If you want to read more about this technique, I highly recommend* **Twist, Turn, & Tie 50 Japanese Kumihimo Braids** *(see page 104) for how-to and lots of braided patterns showcasing this technique.*

A CUP OF JOE

Are you the sort of person whose morning does not begin without that necessary jolt of caffeine? Do you have a designated coffee corner in your kitchen with all of your coffee mugs and gadgets? Do you identify with Lorelai Gilmore and her need for "coffee coffee coffee"?

If so, this pattern is for you!

My stitched-up version is in the colors of fall and immediately calls to mind pumpkin mocha goodness!

This pattern combines fabric appliqué with regular embroidery techniques. The heart-shaped steam and coffee cup are made out of fabric. I then traced and embroidered the saucer directly on the background fabric.

Alter the colors for this pattern to make a coffee-themed hoop for every season: pumpkin spice, peppermint mocha, vanilla latte or freestyle stitch a few cubes and you have an iced coffee!

SNAPSHOT

Photographs can evoke nostalgia for times past. Besides having a really great vintage vibe, with softened and blurred edges, the iconic square shape is great for showcasing your favorite fabrics.

I created this Snapshot pattern to highlight and embellish small squares of fabric. Rather than using large cuts of fabric, this project lets you focus on just one part of the fabric design.

For my project, I envisioned a wall display of photos with a fabric that, for me, embodies the feel of adventure, exploration and travel. Each photo portion of the pattern contains a piece of fabric that I was drawn to and wanted to embellish. For the string displaying your photos, try a new-to-you material — maybe a scrap of thick yarn, a necklace chain, or a silk cord. Use a variety of materials to create fun accents scattered throughout your embroidered pieces.

EMBROIDERY HOOP

Embrace your love of stitching by stitching a fabric embroidery hoop!

This pattern, once again, can be versatile and is open to your own Boho customization! Simply stitch the pattern as is, then place it in an embroidery hoop frame for a hoop within a hoop effect. You can also add to the pattern, as I did in this embroidery hoop wall hanging.

If this were an episode of The Great British Bake Off, this project would be my showstopper!

To make this wall hanging, I used a ready-made burlap linen towel. You can probably find one or something similar at a local craft or home store. To that, I added my embroidery hoop pattern, which I stitched onto a piece of felt. The hoop portion of this pattern uses stitchable cork, which is as thin as fabric and can be used with fusible interfacing. I added a necklace chain around the cork hoop, and then to further embellish, I used floral elements from fabric, vintage ribbon from a dress shop, and seed beads. A fabric-wrapped dowel completes the Boho vibe.

Create a hoop that speaks to your love of embroidery as much as this project speaks to mine!

PATTERNS INSPIRED BY FLORA

I am constantly inspired by the natural world: the saturated colors, the subtle textures, the variety in every leaf and flower. It is a theme that I could embroider over and over again, so much so that I had to restrain myself in the number of patterns that I included in this chapter!

The patterns here reflect the flora that most inspire me. I love knowing that no two will look exactly alike, just as in the world of flowers. The variety that you will create with these patterns will be also have that endless variety of possible beautiful results.

As you begin to plan your flora-inspired stitching, I encourage you to look at fabrics and textures through a different lens. Just as there are beautiful textures in the natural world, there are a variety of fabrics and materials you can use to mimic those textures.

These are small projects that are designed to give you the opportunity to experiment with new textures and stitches. Before starting, take a trip to a local fabric store and see what interesting examples might be hiding out in the remnant bin. Because these patterns don't need yards and yards of fabric, have fun choosing small pieces of vinyl, tulle, velvet or silk to experiment with. You might just find a new favorite material!

HYDRANGEA

Hydrangeas will always hold a special place in my heart. When I see a bouquet of them, I instantly recall my wedding bouquet that I made from sage green and deep violet hydrangeas. From when they are first getting their new flowers, all the way through summer when they are full of intensely colored bold blooms to the muted hues of their flowers in the fall, hydrangeas are a constantly changing palette of inspiration!

I stitched two versions of this pattern to show the variety of textures that can be used to create hydrangea blooms.

The first hoop is the embroidery only version. On a background of gray and neon green, the hydrangea has a stem made from wool roving that is couched to the fabric. Each flower is varied in both color and stitch. I was even able to embroider with a yarn I found that instantly made me think of a light purple hydrangea flower.

The fabric appliqué version of this hoop was enlarged from the pattern by 140%. Some of the flowers have eyelets added to them for variety, and I interspersed bunches of silver and gold sequins among the flowers for a little extra sparkle.

CHINESE LANTERN

This simple pattern makes me think of all things fall!

Another dig through the remnant bin at the fabric store led to an experiment with a textured background for this hoop. A delicate pattern on the ivory background adds visual interest when creating a simple vase, filled with Chinese lantern sprigs.

The texture for the flowers comes from a hand-dyed mixture of silk and velvet scrap pieces. Again, it is really important to test delicate fabrics to see how they will react with heat when adding the fusible interfacing. This is especially true for vintage fabrics. Both the silk and velvet used in this hoop reacted well to the fusible when I placed a scrap piece of fabric between them and the iron.

Have a vintage silk tie or scarf in an autumn, orange color? This is a great project to use pieces of that for the flowers! For added interest without distracting from the pattern, I incorporated seed beads in shades of white.

MONSTERA LEAVES

Monstera leaves have such a classy feel. This plant is versatile enough to fit into both modern or eclectic decor.

To show the variety that can be achieved by decreasing or increasing a pattern size, I stitched up two samples. The first version uses a pattern reduced to 50% of the full-size pattern. Rather than experiment with several fabrics in the smaller size, I embroidered the entire design in black on a colorful fabric background. The holes in the leaves provide a great opportunity to make use of the eyelet stitch.

Using the full-size version of the pattern creates a larger hoop. I wanted the leaves to stand out on this fabric and so used a vinyl remnant for one of the leaves and a shiny leopard print knit for the others.

When experimenting with fabrics other than quilting cotton, it's a good idea to test a small piece with the fusible interfacing to see how it will react. Both of these fabrics worked well, but I did need to iron from the reverse side of the fabrics so that they didn't get scorched by the heat from your hot iron!

COLEUS LEAVES

I was introduced to the coleus plant by my husband, who never fails to find the coolest plants for our jungle of a garden. The leaves remind me of paper that has been splattered with paint in a random pattern. I also appreciate the wide palette of colors in the leaves of this lovely plant.

My Coleus Leaves hoop follows the pattern with the exception of the lines on the leaves. When I was choosing my fabric, I fell in love with a neon green that already had gray lines throughout. As I assembled this pattern, I wasn't sure if I would leave the lines off or stitch them on despite the lines in the fabric. It turns out that I just really liked the effect of the lines that were already on these, and I didn't want to distract by stitching additional lines on top.

You always have the freedom, as I did, to stray from the pattern when you feel like it! Go with what feels right to you as you are working on your project. If you really like the effect you are creating, I hereby give you the freedom to stray from the patterns as much as you want. That is Boho embroidery at its finest!

PATTERN ASSEMBLY TIP: *Rather than cutting out all your interfacing-backed pattern pieces all at once, I recommend cutting out one piece at a time and attaching it to your background fabric, before cutting out another piece. It might seem easier to just cut out all of your pieces and then, like a jigsaw puzzle, figure out how to put them back into place on the fabric. But you will get more accurate results by taking it piece by piece. Learn from my mistakes, and save yourself some frustration!*

AUTUMN BOUQUET AND SUCCULENT

I'm going to be completely honest with you about these next two patterns: They will take a good amount of time to complete, especially if you use the fabric appliqué method. I feel as though you should go into the project with your eyes wide open, knowing these patterns are among the most labor intensive in the book due to the extensive fussy cutting and piecing.

That being said, when you have completely assembled each pattern with all of your scraps of fabric, you must step back, take a look at it, and pat yourself on the back, because the results will be amazing!

If the thought of trying to cut out so many little pieces sounds not one iota enjoyable, then by all means just embroider the pattern directly onto a fabric that you love. Choose a filling stitch such as the satin stitch or a woven stitch, and your end result will be just as amazing because you had a good time stitching it!

These patterns come from my love of succulents and my love of fall colors — and I know I am not alone in loving both things! From the golden hues of yellow and orange to the deep rusts and purples, there is so much variety in the fall garden to re-create in your stitching.

When choosing fabrics for your pattern pieces, look for graduated colors or designs that work well with your embroidery pattern. By adding variety in color or design, you may not need to cut as many individual pieces. For example, in my Autumn Bouquet hoop, I used a striped Flaurie and Finch fabric to add variety to my leaves and was able to cut out the leaves as one piece rather than lots of little pieces. I did the same thing with the sunflower petals. Looking carefully at your fabric choices and utilizing shifts in color, can save you time when fussy cutting.

CELOSIA AND COCKSCOMB

Our wild backyard garden was planted with both cockscomb and celosia some years back. Over time, these two varieties have cross-pollinated, and every spring we have hybrid varieties that come up from seed in the garden. Vivid pinks and purples and sometimes a touch of orange have combined to create a Seuss-like world, just steps from our back door. The combination of these two flowers is the inspiration for this wild floral pattern.

You'll notice that my hoop doesn't follow the placement of the flowers on the original pattern, and that's okay! I encourage you to arrange the pieces from the pattern in whichever way you want. You can match up the pattern exactly or you can freestyle it a little, as I often end up doing, even with my own patterns.

It can be fun to sprinkle in bits of velvet or felt into a project like this. Because these plants are so textural in real life, I wanted to mimic that in my fabric choices for this pattern.

PATTERNS INSPIRED BY FAUNA

I especially love the fact that the patterns in this chapter have been inspired by fauna and are not exact replicas. If you are an ornithologist, entomologist, or lepidopterist, allow me to apologize for adding whimsy and taking liberties with the structure of each of these creatures! The adjustments are intentional and are meant to be a fun take on these creatures. I hope that you will also be inspired to have fun combining fabrics and textures based on the following patterns.

BIRDS ON A WIRE

An avid backyard bird watcher, I love spotting birds sitting high atop wires and buildings while they quietly (and sometimes not so quietly) watch the world below them.

I kept this pattern simple, just the silhouettes of birds on a wire. However, I encourage you to mix up your fabric choices and go with patterns or colors that you normally might not combine. By choosing a large-scale pattern for the background, I was able to include detailed fabrics with smaller patterns for the birds and they still stand out. The outline stitching on the birds also helps them to remain separate from the background fabric. I chose fabrics from the same Joel Dewberry line, so they were designed to complement each other, but you do not necessarily have to do that to get the same patchwork vibe. With a pattern like this, you can go bold for great impact!

STEAMPUNK BEE AND BEETLE

I created these patterns with the purpose of adding steampunk elements to fabric. I love the juxtaposition of sweet floral prints with the industrial feel of gears and clockworks. This is my favorite mixed media project in the whole book because there were so many opportunities to embellish the fabric.

I took several liberties with the pattern design when I created my hoops. You will notice that on the Steampunk Beetle, I added a floral element to its body, rather than follow the pattern design. While you work on this or any of the pattern designs throughout the book, I encourage you to let your fabric choices dictate which lines from the pattern to follow and which not to.

When adding lightweight metal pieces to your project, use white washable glue to hold your pieces in place before you stitch them. It takes only a few drops of glue. Allow the glue to dry and then stitch the embellishment into place.

If steampunk is not your thing, you can stitch these patterns as they are, skipping the gears and watch embellishments completely. I won't tell.

THE HALF-MOTH COLLECTION

The next four patterns are a series that I call the "Half-Moths." I chose moths rather than butterflies because moths have such subtle beauty and texture. I wanted to create a collection that brings them into a quirky limelight, creating a half-moth rather than a full-moth.

Fabric choices are an integral part of this collection. Again, I went with whimsy, over exact replicas of moths, but the essence of these creatures can be reflected in your fabric choices. If you look at pictures of the luna moth, garden tiger moth, rosy maple moth, and cecropia moth, you can get a feel for their incredible natural colors.

Have fun with your stitches too! This would be a great collection to add in the Victorian tufted stitch using silk thread. Many of these moths have fuzzy features in real life, and those details can be highlighted with this fun and textured stitch.

The original design of smaller half-moths can be stitched to fit within a hoop or can be stitched and then stretched onto a canvas, like my version. For a different look, I stitched the smaller versions of the moths in all white. The bunched couching stitch works great for a solid color project like this and reminds me of the apparel designs of Alabama Chanin, both being subtle and highly textured. The alternative design in this collection has each moth occupying their own hoop. Each moth is sized to fit within a 9" hoop when reversed and enlarged to the percentage listed on page 110.

PATTERNS INSPIRED BY PEOPLE

This series of patterns stemmed from my love of giving hand-stitched gifts. There is something so special about creating embroidery projects with someone specific in mind. Spending the time selecting the pattern, choosing the perfect fabrics, and then hand-stitching results in a gift as unique as the recipient.

Each of these patterns can be tailored to suit someone in your life for whom you want to create a unique gift featuring their favorite things.

GIRL WITH CHICKENS

For the farm girl in your life! I don't think I'm alone in my love of chickens. I envisioned this chicken pattern stitched in a variety of my favorite Denyse Schmidt plaid and floral scraps that I've been holding on to for just the right project.

Your version can be simple and stitched onto a solid background with patchwork details or it can simply be outlined using your favorite stitches and not appliquéd at all. There are so many great fabrics that would look adorable with this design. Transferring the pattern to a tea towel would make a perfect hostess or housewarming gift.

DANCER

For the dancer in your life! This pattern was so much fun to create, and there are endless possibilities for dressing up this dancer. Customize the colors to commemorate an upcoming recital or add frills like tulle, sequins, or sparkly ribbon.

Stitch the pattern onto your favorite floral fabric using all-black thread for a simple statement piece. I chose a bold floral as my background fabric, and then back-stitched around the pattern using a size 5 black Eleganza Perle cotton thread.

For a beautiful and also useful gift, perhaps to commemorate a performance, create a drawstring bag to hold a dancer's gear. Use a ready-made tote bag, like I did, or personalize this gift even further by making the bag from scratch too!

SO YOU WANT TO PUT THIS ON A BAG?

STEP 1: Decide on the size of your background fabric. I traced the circle of a hoop larger than the pattern onto fusible interfacing and then transferred that to my background fabric.

STEP 2: Cut out the circle. Do not peel off the paper backing.

STEP 3: Using the fabric appliqué method, transfer your pattern pieces to the background fabric and iron in place.

STEP 4: Once the pieces have all been ironed into place, peel off the backing from the background circle.

STEP 5: Stitch your design. Stitching your design before ironing it to the bag minimizes the wear and tear of threads that are on the inside of your bag.

STEP 6: When you have finished stitching, place the circle on the bag where desired, and iron into place.

STEP 7: Stitch an outline around the patch to secure it, and you have a customized bag!

GARDENER

For the gardener in your life! For every pattern in this book, you have the opportunity to stitch the design exactly as I drew it, creating a work of art that reflects your style in the choices of fabric and embroidery stitches. What a sense of accomplishment you will feel!

However, you can also adjust each pattern to really Boho it up! It wouldn't be Boho embroidery, after all, if I didn't encourage you to break the rules a little bit. I am not a great follower when it comes to patterns (I don't even follow

FUSSY CUTTING TIP: *Rather than fussy cutting the chosen elements from the fabric first and then adding fusible interfacing to the pieces, I highly recommend that you adhere the interfacing to a larger section of the fabric first and then fussy cut the bits of fabric that you want to add to your pattern. It will be so much easier to cut out the tiny little details and to iron them to your fabric!*

my own!) because I enjoy freestyle stitching. One of my favorite things about Boho embroidery is that it gives you the freedom to use the pattern as inspiration rather than a rule book.

I chose this hoop to show you an example of what I mean. When you compare the pattern to my finished hoop, you will see that the main elements are all there in approximately the called-for locations. However, look closely and you will notice fussy cut flowers inside the flower pots rather than hand-stitched flowers and fussy cut leaf branches along the top edge for extra detail.

What other changes would you make? How about adding a few more pots and flowers around your gardener? Or you could eliminate everything but the gardener and add her to a floral background and incorporate embellishments to make it look like a garden. How about adding a bouquet of flowers to every flower pot that sits next to her? Do you see what I mean? Make this pattern your own. Allow yourself to be inspired by the fabric that you choose and create something that makes you happy and is personal to you!

BOOKWORM

For the bookworm in your life! Who doesn't need an extra bag to tote books back and forth from the library or school? Are you in a book club and want to make a special gift for your reading friends? Do you just really love to read and want to declare your love of the written word with a book-themed hoop in your home library?

This pattern can suit all of those needs! Make a customized hoop for yourself or a fellow bookworm. Or, follow the instructions for the Dancer bag, and your library girl is now on her very own tote, ready to watch over all of her books and papers.

IDEAS INSPIRED BY YOU—

THE STITCHER

If you flip ahead a few pages, you will notice that there are no patterns in this chapter. That's right, we've reached the point in the book where I gently give you a few more words of encouragement and then send you off on your own. You are ready to take off the training wheels, to buy a one-way ticket to Hollywood, to grab the machete and face the uncharted jungle, whichever metaphor works for you.

I urge you to expand on your embroidery by creating your own patterns. Yes, I said it: You can create your own embroidery patterns! This is not meant to be an overwhelming endeavor, rather a challenge to take this form of art into your own hands and make it uniquely yours.

So, instead of giving you patterns, how about a few more ideas to use as a starting point for going in your own creative direction?

PATCHES

A fun twist for any embroidery is to create an iron-on or sew-on patch. Remember the fun patches that you decorated your backpack with in your school days? You can embroider your own! Simply adjust the size of any pattern to fit your patch, then print the design and transfer the pattern to the fabric of your choice using one of the methods you learned in this book.

Do you know a teen or tween who might like to be gifted a few hand-sewn patches? This is a quick gift idea that can be personalized for your recipient!

LOCAL INSPIRATION

There is so much to be inspired by on a daily basis. My next idea is to look to what inspires you locally and create a pattern based on that.

I live on the outskirts of Philadelphia, and the idea of creating a Philly Skyline hoop came from my husband, who is always giving me more than enough ideas for things that I should create!

The pattern you create can be as detailed or straightforward as you want it to be. I chose several buildings that I always notice the most and that are iconic to our city skyline.

If the idea of a skyline is too daunting to take on, why not choose to focus on one object that is local to you? The City of Brotherly Love is home to an iconic LOVE statue created by artist Robert Indiana. Creating a pattern based on this statue is a unique way to celebrate a local landmark and have fun with fabric and stitching at the same time.

ARTWORK

My boys are constantly drawing pictures for me that they want me to turn into "stitchings." Kids' creative expressions are a wonderful source for creating an embroidery pattern.

I created two hoops, each from a picture that one of my boys drew for me. I did not rein in their ideas and said I would stitch whatever they drew. With their drawings, I was able to create patterns that I transferred onto fusible interfacing, using the method on page 58. They gave me color suggestions, and then I was free to pick fabrics and embroider their drawings how I wanted.

Imagine the joy this project would bring if you gifted it to a parent or grandparent. This is a unique way to preserve your own child's artistic expression.

LITERATURE INSPIRATION

Do you have a favorite book or character from a book that you would like to base a pattern on? I grew up reading every Lucy Maud Montgomery book I could get my hands on. I read and re-read all of the short story compilations, the stand-alone books, and the series she created. When I decided to create a hoop based on a literary character, it was an easy decision to settle on my beloved Anne of Green Gables.

My Anne with an E hoop includes Anne's signature red braids, her simple straw hat, and one of my favorite quotes from the book.

There is so much variety to choose from when creating a pattern like this. I love working with patterns that are meaningful, and this one stirs up all sorts of fond memories for me.

MOVIE AND TELEVISION INSPIRATION

We all have a favorite show or movie that we eagerly settle into and watch over and over again. I could rattle off a handful of comedy series that I love, but when I wanted to create a pattern based on a series, I immediately chose Downton Abbey. Although the Dowager gets to deliver the one-liners that are memorable and memed, Lady Mary gets to wear the fashion that was most fun for me to re-create.

This hoop is a portrait pattern that I created using fabric from the Downton Abbey line from Andover Fabrics. It just felt appropriate to choose fabrics based on photos of Lady Mary and, yes, I embroidered her while watching the show!

What favorite show or movie inspires you? Choose a character or scene and sketch out a drawing that you can use as a pattern.

These are just a handful of ideas to get you started on the road to creating your own patterns. If you are worried that you do not have enough skills, I suggest checking out a book from the library on drawing or even taking a class at your local art center or from an online source such as Creativebug.com. You will feel more confident in your own abilities in no time.

BOHO—iNG ON!

I've given you a lot to work with here, haven't I! Now, where to start?

Choose a pattern that speaks to you. Decide on your method for transferring the pattern. If you are very new to embroidery, simply transfer the pattern to a piece of fabric and begin by learning an embroidery stitch or two. Continue stitching and you will soon see that you can embroider, and your skills will grow and your stitches will become practiced and comfortable. The next project you take on will seem even simpler!

If you already are an embroiderer, try the next step of combining fabric appliqué with embroidery. Choose a pattern, go through your fabric stash, assemble and then get to stitching!

Are you a skilled embroiderer so combining fabric doesn't intimidate you? Great! Take on the challenge of creating your own pattern.

Choose something meaningful to you. You will be spending a lot of time with this pattern, so invest in your efforts and you will be proud of creating something you love.

Expand your stitching palette and add textures that might be new to you. You may just find a new favorite thread or fall in love with velvet or beads. Put together a practice hoop and challenge yourself to try a more complicated stitch.

Remember, this is supposed to be enjoyable. No one is grading you on how your stitches look. Are you happy with it? Are you excited to be learning a new skill? Then that's all that matters! Enjoy the free-spirited approach of Boho embroidery. Play by the rules when appropriate, but bend them when the inspiration strikes.

I'm so excited you have taken the hand-stitching journey with me. Now, go get stitching!

RESOURCES AND SUPPLIES

THREADS

>> Sue Spargo Eleganza Perle Cotton by Wonderfil Threads

>> Dala Pearl Cotton
suespargo.com

>> Sulky Petites
sulky.com

>> Silk 'n Colors
threadgatherer.com

>> Koigu KPM (Premium Merino) Needlepoint Yarn
koigu.com
purlsoho.com

>> Madeline Tosh Unicorn Tails
madelinetosh.com

FUZZY STUFF

>> Very Velvet
rainbowgallery.com

SUPPLIES

>> Richard Hemming & Son
colonialneedle.com

>> Tula Pink 4" Large Ring Micro-Tip Scissors
ihearttulapink.com

>> Fiskars Micro-Tip Easy Action Scissors
fiskars.com

>> WEFTY Needle
tjaye.com

>> The Loome
theloome.com

>> The Beadsmith Kumihimo Disk
beadsmith.com

>> Daylight Wafer Lightbox
daylightcompany.com

>> Sulky Iron-On Transfer Pen

>> Sulky Printable Stick 'n Stitch
sulky.com

>> DMC Stitchable Cork

>> DMC Stitchable Mesh
dmc.com

>> Dritz Mark-B-Gone Marking Pen
dritz.com

>> HeatnBond Lite
thermowebonline.com

>> Bunka Brush
suespargo.com

>> Darice ¾" mirrors
darice.com

>> Stamping Blanks
impressart.com

>> Recollections Metal Embellishments
michaels.com

>> Clover Straight Tailor's Awl
clover-usa.com

>> LLamarama Steel Pencil Case
knitpicks.com

>> Needleminders
etsy.com/shop/
SeptemberHouse
alisonglass.com

BOOKS

>> *Color Inspirations: More than 3,000 Innovative Palettes from the Colourlovers.Com Community*
by Darius A Monsef IV

>> *How to Draw Modern Florals: An Introduction to the Art of Flowers, Cacti, and More*
by Alli Koch

>> *Twist, Turn, & Tie 50 Japanese Kumihimo Braids: A Beginner's Guide to Making Braids for Beautiful Cord Jewelry*
By Beth Kemp

>> *Bead Embroidery Stitch Samples*
by CRK Design and Yasuko Endo

MY FAVORITE SHOPS

Needlework Supplies and Yarn

» **Gazebo Plus**
New Hope, PA
gazeboplus.com

» **Conversational Threads Fiber Arts Studio**
Emmaus, PA
conversationalthreads.com

» **Purl Soho**
New York, NY
purlsoho.com

Fabric

» **Alewives Fabrics**
Nobleboro, ME
alewivesfabrics.com

» **Pennington Quilts**
Pennington, NJ
penningtonquilts.com

» **Hawthorne Threads**
hawthornethreads.com

Beads

» **Fusion Beads**
fusionbeads.com

Reference Websites

» **Mary Corbet's Needle 'n Thread**
needlenthread.com

» **Nordic Needle**
nordicneedle.net

» **Alabama Chanin**
alabamachanin.com

» **Pinterest**
pinterest.com

» **Creativebug**
creativebug.com

» **Spoonflower**
spoonflower.com

THE PATTERNS

Bookworm
(Enlarge 145%)

Girl with Chickens
(Actual Size)

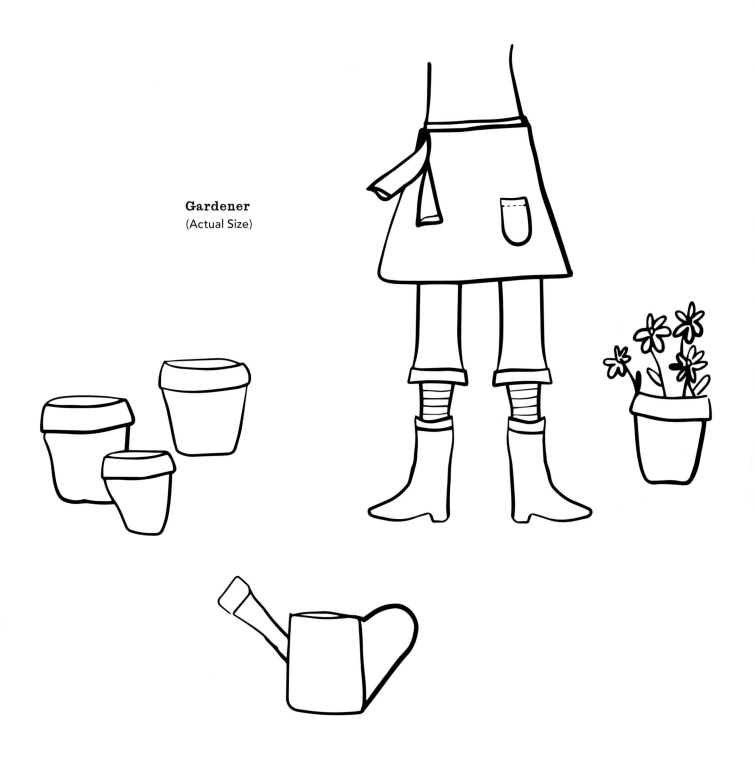

Gardener
(Actual Size)

Steampunk Bee
(Enlarge 110%)

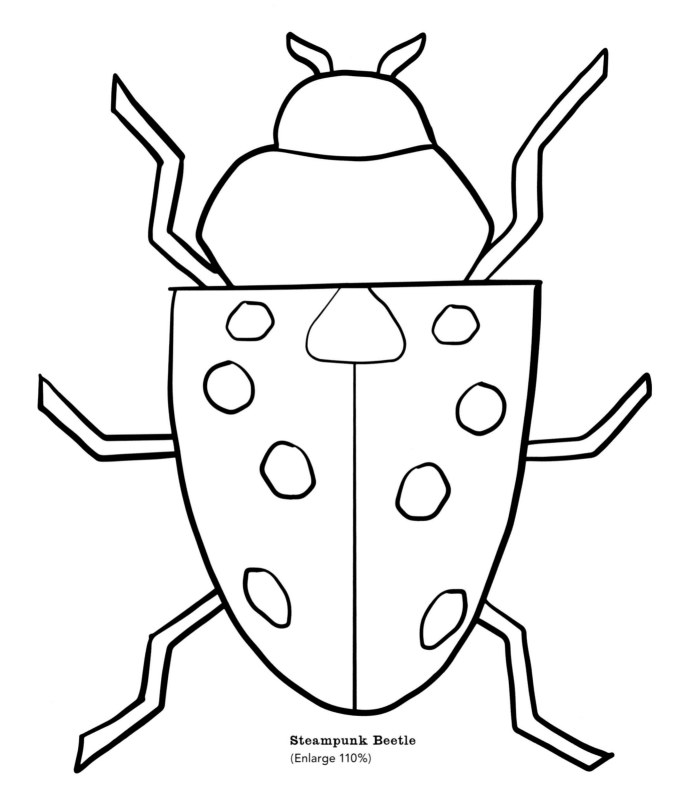

Steampunk Beetle
(Enlarge 110%)

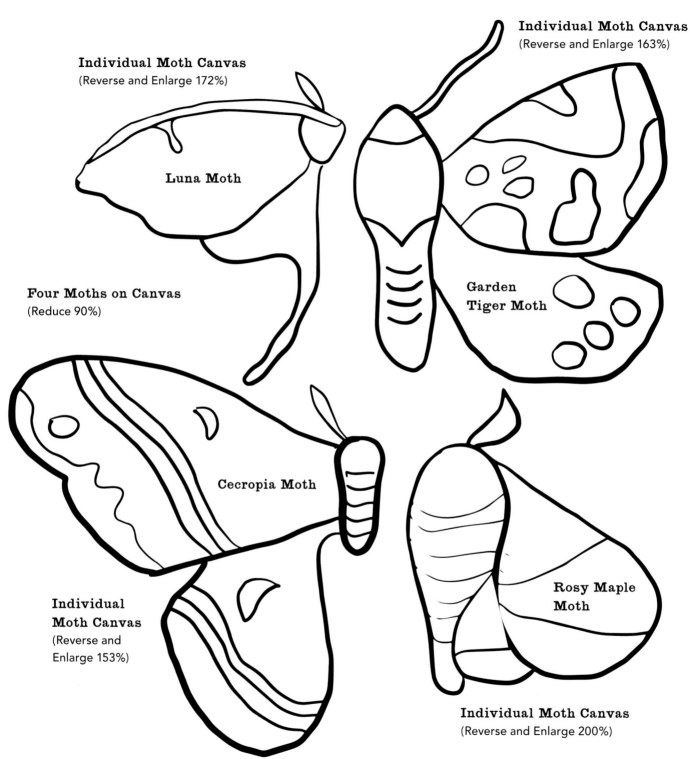

Individual Moth Canvas
(Reverse and Enlarge 172%)

Luna Moth

Individual Moth Canvas
(Reverse and Enlarge 163%)

Four Moths on Canvas
(Reduce 90%)

Garden
Tiger Moth

Cecropia Moth

Individual
Moth Canvas
(Reverse and
Enlarge 153%)

Rosy Maple
Moth

Individual Moth Canvas
(Reverse and Enlarge 200%)

Succulent
(Enlarge 200%)

Autumn Bouquet
(Enlarge 125%)

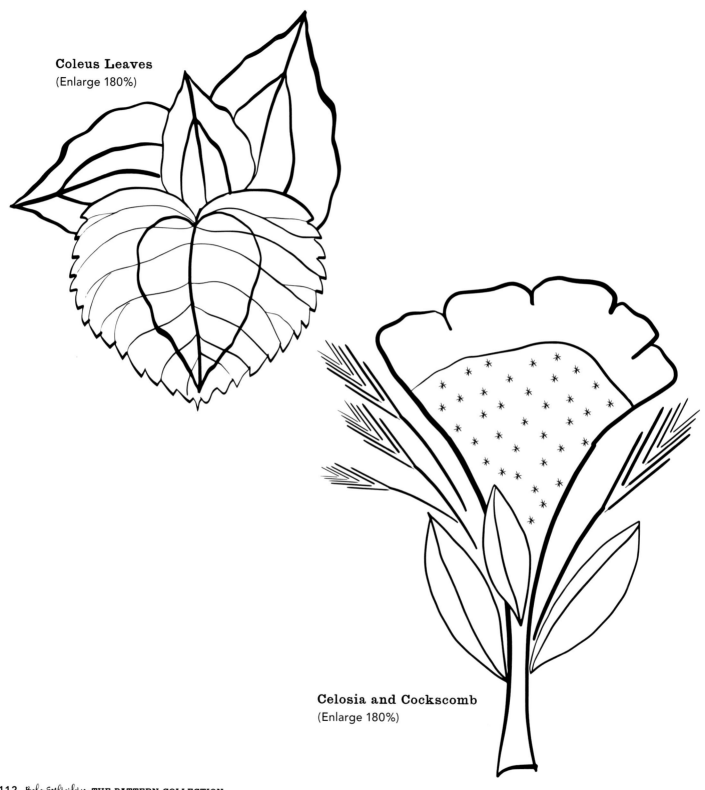

Coleus Leaves
(Enlarge 180%)

Celosia and Cockscomb
(Enlarge 180%)

Chinese Lantern
(Enlarge 115%)

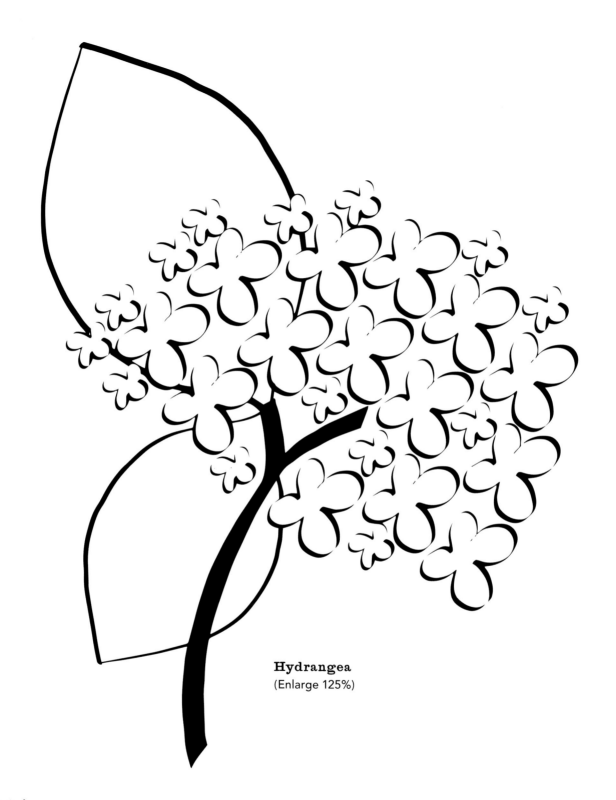

Hydrangea
(Enlarge 125%)

Monstera Leaves
(Enlarge 125%)

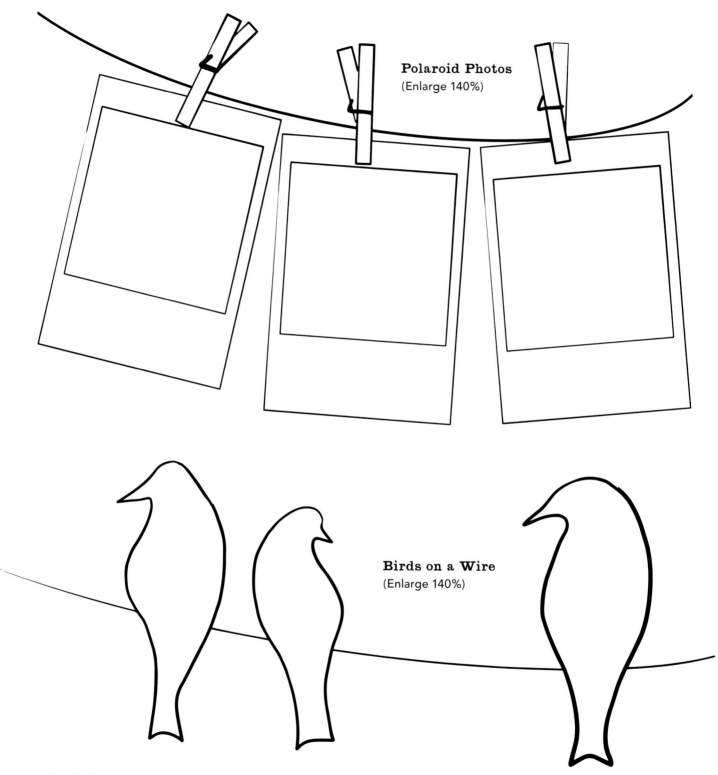

Polaroid Photos
(Enlarge 140%)

Birds on a Wire
(Enlarge 140%)

Embroidery Hoop
(Enlarge 110%)

Coffee Cup
(Actual Size)

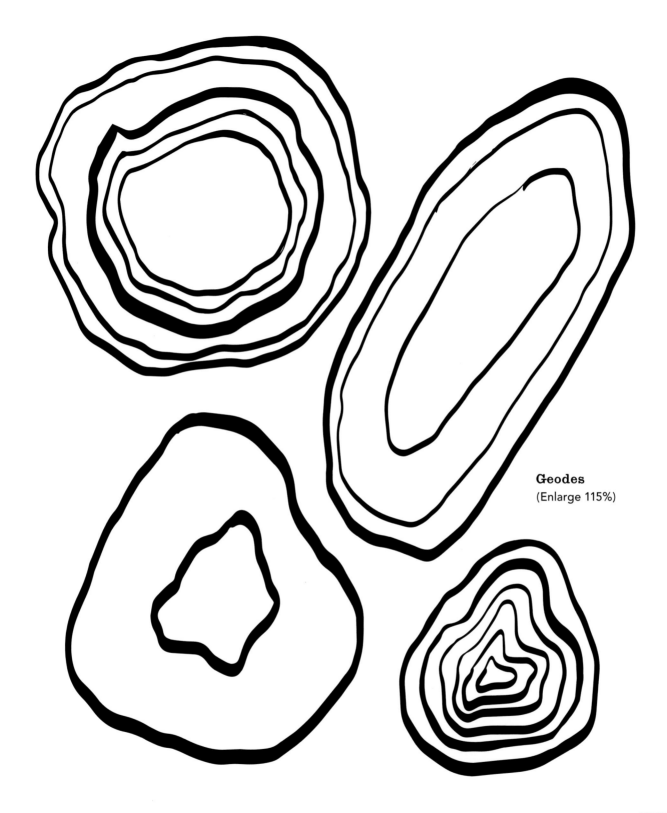

Geodes
(Enlarge 115%)

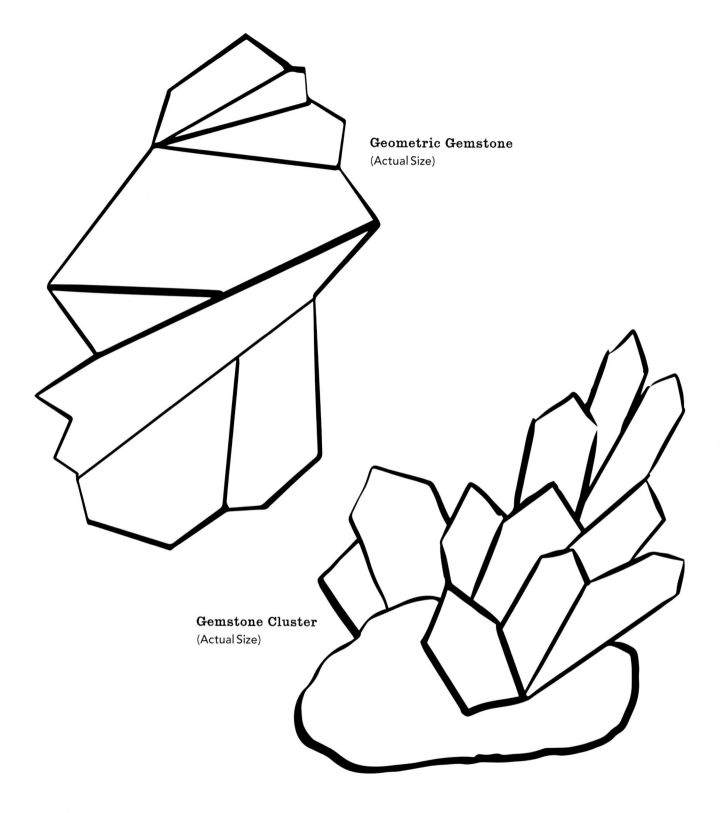

Geometric Gemstone
(Actual Size)

Gemstone Cluster
(Actual Size)

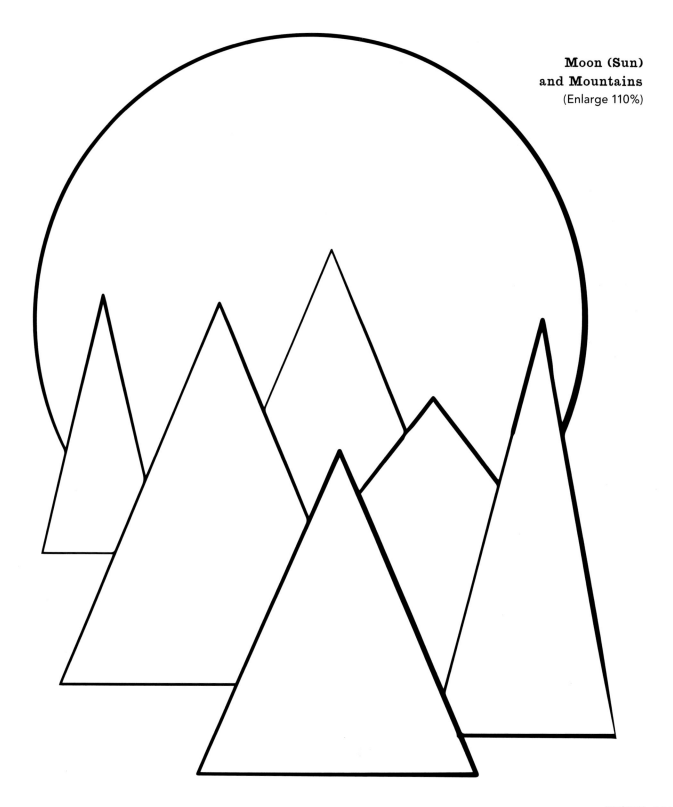

**Moon (Sun)
and Mountains**
(Enlarge 110%)

**Stained Glass
Pineapple**

(Enlarge 110%)

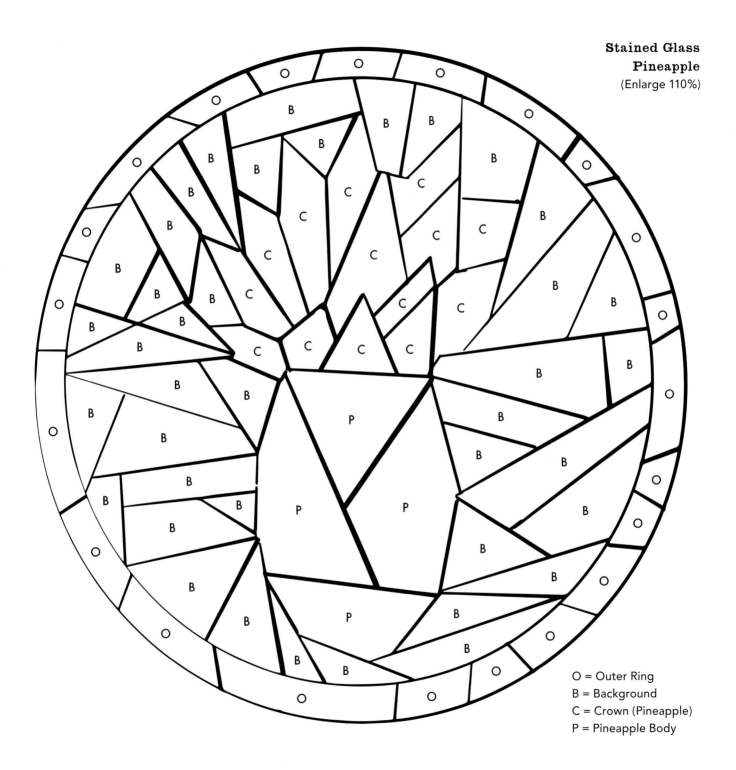

Stained Glass
Pineapple
(Enlarge 110%)

O = Outer Ring
B = Background
C = Crown (Pineapple)
P = Pineapple Body

**Stained Glass
Tranquil Fields**

(Enlarge 110%)

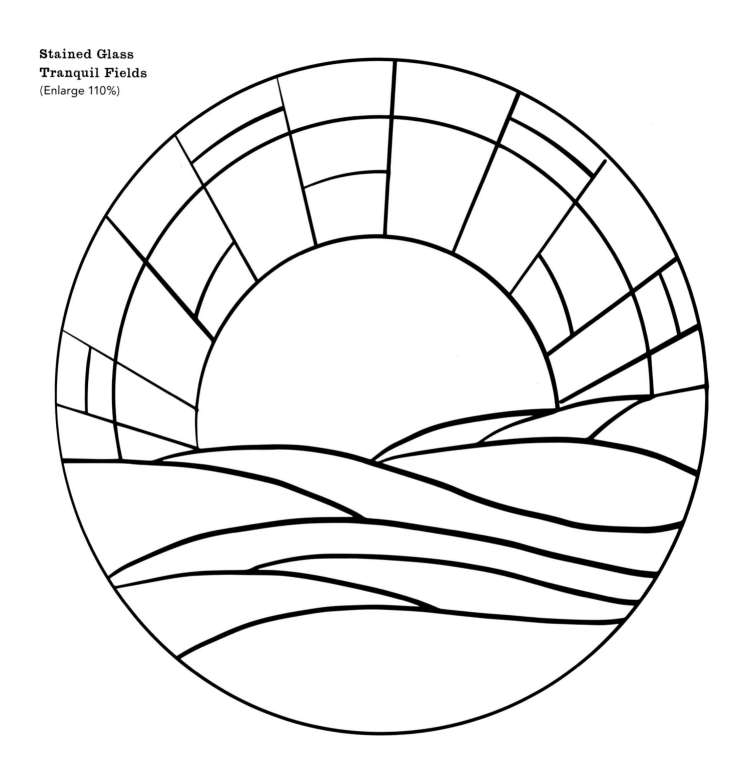

**Stained Glass
Choppy Waters**
(Enlarge 110%)

Hot Air Balloons
(Enlarge 115%)

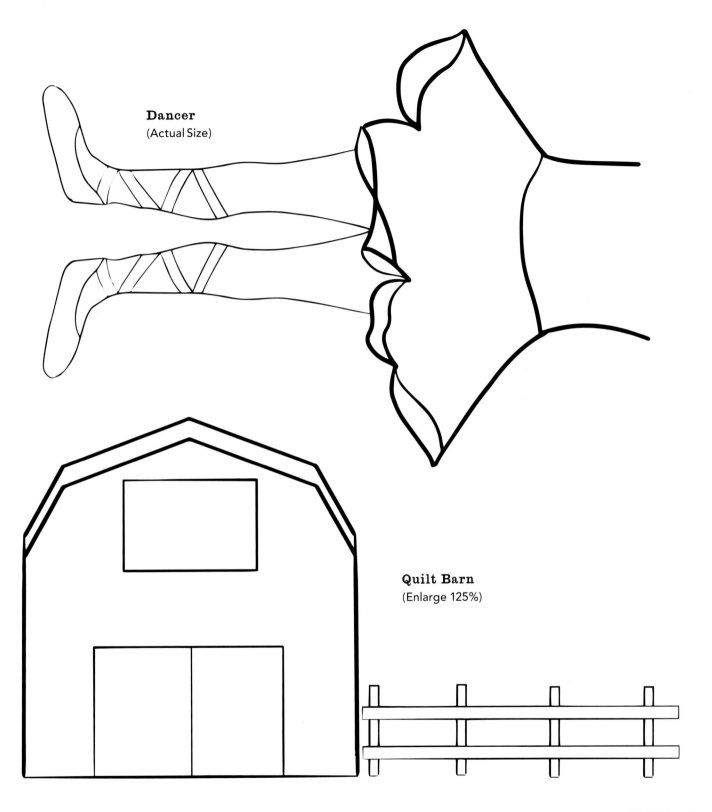

Dancer
(Actual Size)

Quilt Barn
(Enlarge 125%)